C000091471

*The BA*1
of Holistic
Horse Medicine and
Management

Keith Allison

Senior Veterinary Adviser
Christopher Day

COMPASS EQUESTRIAN
LONDON

First published in Great Britain in 1998 by
Compass Equestrian Limited

© Keith Allison 1998

No part of this book may be reproduced
or transmitted in any way or by any means,
electronic, or mechanical, including photocopy,
recording, or any information storage or retrieval
system, without permission in writing from the publishers.
All rights reserved.

ISBN 1 900667 57 6

A catalogue record for this book is available
from the British Library

Printed in Egypt
by
International Printing House, Cairo

Illustrations by Maggie Raynor
Edited by Martin Diggle
Cover design by Hugh Johnson

CONTENTS

LIST OF COLOUR ILLUSTRATIONS

These are denoted in the text by $\boxed{\text{I}}$ ▶ next to the relevant entry.

PREFACE

The BAHNM Dictionary of Holistic Horse Medicine and Management draws on both modern scientific and technical research and on historical references to provide in one volume a compendium of information on equine physiology, nutrition, biochemistry, common diseases and holistic veterinary therapies.

Many reference works on subject-matter of this type tend to be either 'conventional' or 'alternative' in tone, each excluding terms and information which they deem irrelevant to their own particular philosophy. A great deal of common ground and improved mutual understanding can needlessly be missed through this approach. Therefore, in this dictionary, information is provided which will allow the reader to relate one discipline or philosophy usefully to another. The author also intends to provide signposts to further research, which in addition to increasing the reader's knowledge in specific technical areas will also serve to allow traditional and modern practices to be compared and evaluated.

This dictionary will be an invaluable source of reference for horse owners wishing to apply holistic methods to equine management; for equine nutritionists and therapists; for students of veterinary science or animal husbandry, and for anyone seeking information on holistic equine nutrition and medicine.

ABOUT THE BAHNM

The BAHNM (British Association of Holistic Nutrition and Medicine) promotes the use of nutritional products and medicinal therapies which are compatible with the principles of holism. Holism is a philosophy founded on the belief that all systems in nature are part of a whole and that disruption to any part of the system, no matter how small, has the potential to disrupt the integrity of the whole. While this concept has been appreciated in many cultures through the ages, it was Jan Christian Smutts (1870—1950) who enabled it to be understood in modern scientific terms. Holism can be demonstrated in all matter and at all levels, from the individual cell to the most complex biological systems. A simple but highly significant example of holism is the behaviour of the individual cells of a living organism, which operate for the benefit of the whole being.

A major part of the work of the BAHNM is to broaden the scientific understanding of the inextricable link between nutrition and medicine. This association is not a recent revelation; it has been recognised in the West since the days of the Greek physician Hippocrates (c.460-380 BC), whose work was so influential that he is regarded as 'the father of modern medicine' (indeed, the Hippocratic oath bears his name). Hippocrates' approach to medicine was radically different from the ideas of his contemporaries, whose treatments he saw as little more than witchcraft. He himself took a more pragmatic approach, believing that in order to effect a proper cure it was necessary to take into consideration the cause of a problem as well as the symptoms. As part of his work, he studied the effects that various foods had on the body, and advocated the use of diet and plant medicines to prevent and cure disease. His maxim: 'Let food be thy medicine and medicine thy food' is just as relevant today as it has always been.

While Hippocrates' ideas of 'holistic' treatment were perceived as radical in his day, the use of many of the substances he employed to treat ailments can be traced even further back into history. For example, the medicinal use of herbs, for which he is perhaps best known, had been practised in other cultures from a much earlier time. The famous *Elbers Papyrus*, an Egyptian document dating from circa 1500 BC, contains information on some 365 herbal remedies; and an even older document, *The Shen Nung Herbal*, originated by the Chinese Emperor Shen Nung circa 2700 BC, lists many plant medicines. It is remarkable that some of the medicines in use today are the same as, or based upon, materials which were being prescribed 5000 years ago.

Despite such continuity, there was a decline in the use of herbal medicines and other natural therapies as the modern pharmaceutical industry expanded in the middle of the twentieth century. Today, however, there is a renewed interest in holistic medicine and nutrition, which is prompted mainly by the problems associated with products of the modern, polarised, biological sciences. The inherent risk of using modern technological products is that the advantages may be outweighed by the disadvantages. All modern synthetic drugs and manufactured pharmaceutical compounds carry a risk of injurious side-effects, some of which may become apparent only after long-term use.

Even 'natural' raw materials are not without risk if they are used unwisely — as the unfortunate consequence of feeding animal by-products to herbivores has shown in the form of Bovine Spongiform Encephalopathy (BSE) in cattle.

One difficulty which should be addressed for the common good is the polarisation of medical philosophies. Protagonists of natural methods are often perceived as idealists, for whom the world must stop. Conversely, modern science is often seen as relentlessly determined to push forward with new technologies, forever debunking traditional methods along the way. The truth is that the open-minded practitioners of both methodologies are learning from each other, often with beneficial results. On the one hand, for example, new cancer treatments are being derived from natural medicines in use amongst tribal cultures in the Amazonian rain forests; on the other hand, modern science has shown that some traditional remedies carry their own dangers and should be discontinued — as with the use of turpentine as an anthelmintic.

What should be learned from this is that the benefits lie in co-operation between the medical philosophies. The BAHNM believes that a dogged determination to follow either philosophy to the exclusion of the other is wrong, and that the best interests of medicine will be served by a balanced approach, whereby the discoveries of modern science are put to use in a way which is more compatible with natural principles.

That said, the BAHNM sees a duty to correct misconceptions which may muddy comparison between 'traditional' and 'modern' approaches. It is, for example, a common misconception that traditional medicines such as herbs are not 'robust' enough to counter many serious diseases — an attitude which perhaps stems from the fact that many people nowadays associate the term 'herb' primarily with food seasoning. The truth, however, is rather different: consider, for instance, the physiological effects of the opiate drugs derived fom the poppy. Furthermore,while it is true that a good deal of holistic medicine is concerned with preventative therapy, it is also the case that many veterinarians are able to use holistic medicines and methods almost to the exclusion of technological drug therapy.

There is also a common belief that it is impossible to formulate feeds for the modern horse without using laboratory-produced vitamins and other additives. However, what is forgotten is that horses were working just as hard (if not harder) in the service of man for many generations before vitamins had even been identified. All the nutrients required for equine nutrition are available from natural sources — it is simply a case of using the appropriate raw materials.

Thus the BAHNM promotes the use of natural materials both in feedstuffs and in medicines, where they provide a viable alternative to modern technological products. This is on the basis that such products are more compatible with the evolved requirements of the species, and that they are therefore less likely to cause physiological or mental problems or side-effects. To this end, the BAHNM provides advice on holistic nutrition and medicine to horse owners, and disseminates information to those involved in the provision of animal nutrition and health-care services to the public.

The BAHNM is also a source of information concerning the different types of natural therapies available, together with the legal aspects of therapeutic practice. It maintains a register of properly qualified and experienced holistic practitioners, including saddlers and saddle fitters, and also administers the licensing procedure for holistic products in collaboration with the appropriate government departments and regulatory bodies, chiefly the Ministry of Agriculture, the Trading Standards Department, the Veterinary Medicines Directorate and The Royal College of Veterinary Surgeons. In order to become licensed, products must be manufactured to the *Quality Standard for Holistic Products*, which applies strict criteria to manufacturing methods, ingredients and quality control.

ABOUT THE AUTHOR

Keith Allison is from an agricultural background which reflected more traditional and sustainable methods of husbandry than those practised in today's increasingly intensive farming industry. In 1970, he joined a multi-national veterinary pharmaceutical company, and went on to gain substantial technical experience in product development in the animal health and food industries.

He now works closely with researchers and practitioners in the field of holistic nutrition and medicine, and is a prominent exponent of holistic methods of animal husbandry and management, together with the health and welfare benefits that these methods provide. He is the author of several books on the subject.

As Secretary of the British Association of Holistic Nutrition and Medicine, he is involved in furthering the Association's aims and objectives, providing advice and information for consumers, and collaborating with various regulatory bodies in the administration of the *Licensing Procedure for Holistic Products*.

ABOUT THE VETERINARY ADVISER

Christopher Day, a veterinary surgeon whose parents were also veterinarians, was introduced to holistic medicine at an early age. After qualifying at Downing College, Cambridge in 1972 he, in turn, entered the profession and is now a leading specialist in holistic equine medicine. He is consulted world-wide on animal welfare and is involved in many environmental and wildlife issues. His approach to treatment involves properly integrated holistic therapies, including homoeopathy, nutritional therapy, herbal medicine, acupuncture and physiotherapy.

He has served as Chairman to various holistic veterinary organisations, both in England and abroad, and as Veterinary Dean to the Faculty of Homoeopathy he is actively involved in the training of veterinary surgeons in post-graduate qualifications. He is the author of several books on holistic veterinary medicine, and senior veterinary adviser to the BAHNM.

ACKNOWLEDGEMENTS

A substantial amount of information in this dictionary has been obtained from research into traditional methods of horse management, using historical material contained in books and documents from many sources. Cross-references have been made where appropriate from the following modern works: *Black's Medical Dictionary, Chamber's Twentieth Century Dictionary, Collins Dictionary of Medicine, Encyclopaedia Britannica, Oxford Medical Dictionary.*

The author also wishes to thank the following for help and guidance: Caroline Beaney, Joan Carter, Colin Kimber, Matthew Whall, The Ministry of Agriculture, Fisheries and Food, The Royal College of Veterinary Surgeons, The Trading Standards Department, The Veterinary Medicines Directorate. Christopher Day has given permission for the use of certain extracts from two of his own books: *The Homoeopathic Treatment of Small Animals* and *The Homoeopathic Treatment of Beef and Dairy Cattle.*

INTRODUCTION

Since the middle of the twentieth century there have been remarkable advances in the biological sciences.In the light of these, until a few years ago the word of those involved in medicine and nutrition was rarely questioned. Today, however, the scientific community is under the critical gaze of consumers, who are often influenced by people quick to criticise mistakes and slow to acknowledge achievements. The net result of this criticism — whether it is justified or not — is that there is generally more interest in what are often known as 'alternative' methods of nutrition and medicine, both for ourselves and for the animals in our care. As a consequence, the market place for nutritional and medicinal products and services is changing; there is an increasing demand for more wholesome nutritional products and also for the services of healthcare professionals who use holistic methods and therapies.

The demand for such products and services is, in fact, outstripping the legitimate supply, which unfortunately leads to instances of inferior and often illegal products and practices being offered.This not only brings the whole area of 'alternative' methodologies into disrepute — it also represents potential danger to users and their animals.

Current legislation on medicines and feedstuffs is detailed, cumbersome and difficult to apply in certain areas, and there are those who would like to completely 'rewrite the book'. However, it is noticeable that those who push hardest to do this tend to be commercially involved and have the most to gain.The consensus amongst less self-interested observers is that although there are many loopholes in current legislation (mainly because it has not kept pace with the changing market), it is basically sound. Such opinion suggests that, in general, the best course of action by which to provide the consumer with increased protection would be to apply existing legislation more vigorously. What is to be avoided is a relaxation of existing laws, which could open the floodgates for various forms of commercial and professional malpractice.

Whatever the flaws in current legislation, whether in the *Veterinary Surgeons Act*, the *Feeding Stuffs Regulations* or the *Medicines Acts*, we should not lose sight of the fact that these regulations exist primarily to protect animals — in our context, the horse. Any changes which may have a bearing on the health and welfare of these creatures should be made in consultation with those best placed to give independent and well-informed advice — members of the veterinary profession.

Outside the veterinary profession there are many therapists who are educated in various disciplines; these people may, or may not, be competent in their particular sphere of activity. Their level of competence does not, however, transcend the law, which states that only veterinary surgeons may be consulted for the diagnosis and treatment of sick animals. Other therapists — together with those in allied occupations, such as nutritionists — may work only under the direct supervision of a veterinary surgeon. There are very good reasons for this: the hardest task for any veterinary surgeon is correct diagnosis and an unqualified person, despite the best of intentions and considerable experience, is even more likely to misinterpret the symptoms and diagnose incorrectly or incompletely. Delay in obtaining correct treatment can cause serious harm, unnecessary pain, or even death.

At this point it should be emphasised that holistic medicine is an approach to healing which takes into consideration everything that may have a bearing on the case: when all aspects have been assessed against the symptoms, a suitable course of action may be decided upon. This may involve the use of several therapeutic disciplines rather than a prescription for one particular drug, as is often the case with the modern technological approach to medicine.

It is important to appreciate that many of the therapies employed in holistic medicine are not systems of medicine in their own right, and that they must be correctly integrated in order to bring about a cure. This can only be done properly (and legally) by a veterinary surgeon, who is in the best position to orchestrate the treatment. Apart from the legal aspect, the exclusion of properly experienced veterinary

11

management has practical drawbacks. In some cases, whilst therapy may be giving symptomatic relief, it may also be masking problems which could become compounded, leading to more serious trouble later. It is possible, for example, that a physiotherapist might develop muscles in a horse's back without attention being given to the underlying cause of the problem, which may be disease or injury, a badly-fitting saddle, or numerous other things. In other cases, it may be that a different approach will remove the need for therapy altogether. An example of this would be that, if proper nutrition were provided, there would be little need to supplement a horse's diet with herbs, many of which are fundamentally medicinal in action and inappropriate for a horse to ingest on a regular basis without medical justification.

Horse owners who are especially attracted to certain 'alternative' therapies should not, therefore, allow such attractions to cloud their judgement, or prejudice them against members of the veterinary profession who do not practice holistic medicine. They should take note that, whilst natural medicine is not part of the curriculum for veterinary students, many veterinarians are studying the subject after qualifying. There are, for example, post-graduate courses available in veterinary homoeopathy, leading to a recognised qualification, and it seems likely that other organised routes for study will be available in due course

Finally, on this note, it should be emphasised that, if veterinary methods adjudged as holistic are not readily available, other veterinary attention should be sought, to ensure that suffering is not caused or continued by the neglect of painful or distressing symptoms. *An enthusiasm for holistic methods should not be allowed to contribute to poor animal welfare.*

USEFUL ADDRESSES

ADAS (Food Farming, Land and Leisure). *see* Local Directories.

British Association of Holistic Nutrition and Medicine (BAHNM). Borough Court, Hartley Wintney, Basingstoke, Hants RG27 8JA. Tel. 01252 843282.

British Association of Homoeopathic Veterinary Surgeons. Alternative Medicine Centre, Chinham House, Stanford in the Vale, Faringdon, Oxon SN7 8NQ. Tel. 01367 710 324

British Veterinary Association. 7 Mansfield Street, London W1M 0AT. Tel. 0171 636 6541

Ministry of Agriculture, Fisheries and Food. Ergon House, c/o Nobel House, 17 Smith Square, London SW1P 3RJ. Tel. 0171 238 3000.

Royal College of Veterinary Surgeons. 32 Belgrave Square, London SW1 8QP. Tel. 0171 222 2001 (Membership).

The Soil Association. 86 Colston Street, Bristol BS1 5BB. Tel. 0117 9290661.

American Holistic Veterinary Association. Dr. C. Ticket, 2214 Old Emmerton Road, Bel Air, Maryland, 21014. USA

International Veterinary Acupuncture Society. 268 West Third, PO BOX 2094, Boulder CO 80456. USA

Herb Research Foundation. 1007 Pearl St, Suite 200, Boulder CO 80302. USA

National Herbalist Association of Astralia. 27 Leith St, Coorparoo, Queensland, 4151.

IMPORTANT NOTE AND CAUTION

Entries in this dictionary do not constitute advice on treatment. Some entries include information on traditional methods of horse management involving the use of materials and methods which, by today's standards, may be regarded as inappropriate, dangerous, or cruel. This applies especially to many of the traditional remedies for various ailments, some of which may be damaging or even fatal in the wrong hands. It should be emphasised that all but the most minor health problems should be referred to a veterinary surgeon and that remedies for home treatment should be restricted to the use of familiar home medicines. In particular, experimentation with some of the substances described is to be discouraged.

The diagnosis and treatment of sick animals is restricted by Act of Parliament to veterinary surgeons, and they alone should be consulted in the event of disease or injury. It is illegal for persons who are not veterinary surgeons to diagnose and treat sick animals; all other therapists and practitioners must work under the direction of a qualified veterinary surgeon.

This fact will be acknowledged by legitimate complementary medical therapists

The BAHNM maintains a register of properly qualified and experienced holistic practitioners and dissociates itself from activities not in accordance with the above.

Abortifacient A term used (especially in herbal medicine) to describe a substance which causes premature expulsion of a foetus, referred to in earlier times as an emmenogogue. Many herbs have the potential for damage to an unborn foal, and in general none should be given to pregnant mares unless they have been professionally cleared as safe.

Abortion Loss of the foal before 300 days of gestation. Common causes are viral and bacterial infections, twinning, hormonal disturbances, abnormalities of the foal and nutritional problems.

Abrams, Albert see **Radionics**.

Abscess A localised collection of pus. A veterinary surgeon should be consulted for all abscesses, unless they are of the simplest nature.

Acacia catechu see **Catechu**.

Acetate of ammonia A chemical preparation formerly used as an expectorant.

Acetate of lead A chemical preparation formerly used as an astringent. Also used as a dressing for skin erruptions such as eczema and pruritis.

Acetic acid Formerly used as an astringent, corrosive and vesicant. Popular for the removal of warts — see also **Vinegar**.

Achillea millefolium see **Yarrow**.

Acid firing see **Firing**.

Aconite *(Aconitum napellus)* see **Monk's Hood.**

Acorns The fruit of the oak *(Quercus)*, a tree found in most parts of the British Isles. Although horses do sometimes eat acorns with no apparent ill-effects, there have been cases of poisoning in certain circumstances. These have been reported during particularly dry summers when there was a large crop of acorns and other food was scarce. Acorns are listed as poisonous.

Active principle A term used to describe the constituent of a herb or other medicine which is judged to be the most effective from a pharmacological standpoint. Modern drugs typically contain these constituents either in a purified or, possibly, synthesised form. Example of this are asprin and digoxin. Herbal pharmacologists argue that the whole herb provides a much safer and more beneficial interaction than can be provided by the use of individual isolates.

Acupressure Manual stimulation of specific points in the meridian lines of the body for a medicinal purpose. Compare **Acupuncture**.

| I ▶ | **Acupuncture** The science of affecting the functions of the body for a medicinal purpose by the insertion of needles into the body. Acupuncture needles are different from the familiar hypodermic needles in that they are solid and rather finer. They are extremely flexible, usually being made from steel, although other materials such as gold, silver or copper are used.

The needles are placed at specific sites called acupuncture points, which are located in various parts of the body along what are called meridians or energy channels. There is little discomfort experienced by the patient during the treatment, and most horses show signs of great relaxation; some even become drowsy.

Acupuncture has been part of Eastern medicine for many thousands of years and it is now finding favour in Great Britain and other parts of the world for the treatment of many equine ailments. However, it is not regarded as a treatment in its own right, but as a therapy which, when integrated with others, especially herbs, may be used to re-balance the energy flow, known as Qi (pronounced 'chee'), within the body. This form of medicine should only be prac-tised by a veterinary surgeon.

Acute Describes a disease of rapid onset, and brief duration: compare **Chronic**.

Adaptogenic A term used (especially in herbal medicine) to describe a substance which helps to restore the balance within the body. Such remedies improve the body's adapt-ability, in that it is more able to fend off the various ailments with which it comes into contact.

Additive When used in relation to feedstuffs, this term normally means a synthetic substance which has been added to the basic ingredients in order to support artificially the nutritional viability of the feedstuff and also, in the case of meat animals, to increase growth rate and/or production. This practice is not in keeping with holistic nutrition — see **Holistic feeding stuffs and supplements**, **Nutritional supplements**.

Adeno virus see **Rhinovirus**.

Adjuvant A substance used in conjunction with another in order to increase its activity.

Adrenalin An important hormone secreted by the adrenal gland and released into the body as a direct response to fear and/or excitement. It has a specific effect on circulation, sugar metabolism and muscle function.

Adulterants (in feeds) A term used in the animal feed industry to describe inferior or spurious ingredients that have been added to the ration.

Aerobe An organism which relies on free oxygen for survival.

Compare **Anaerobe**.

Aerobic exercise see **Exercise**.

Aesthesia Literally, feeling or perception (aesthetic = of the senses), hence anaesthesia (loss of sensation).

Aetiology The cause of a disease, or the study of such causes.

Afterbirth see **Placenta**.

Age It is often stated that the modern horse is able to live longer than his predecessors because of the development of modern medicines and feedstuffs. This may be a distorted view. One of the reasons why the life expectancy of horses was lower in former times is that most were destroyed at a relatively early age because they were worn out through overwork. However, instances are on record of animals reaching the ages of 35 and 50 and, exceptionally, there was a carthorse on the canal at Warrington who lived to the age of 63.

Youatt (1776-1847), a highly respected veterinary surgeon, reported three horses who died at the ages of 35, 37, and 39. Of the 15 famous racehorses listed by F.Smith in his *Veterinary Physiology*, including such names as the great Eclipse, 11 horses survived to 26 years and beyond, the two oldest being Parrot and Pocahontas, who died at 36 and 33 years respectively.

When assessing the benefits or otherwise of the modern fragmented approach to nutrition, it should be borne in mind that many of the ingredients used on a regular basis have not undergone 'lifetime studies' in the horse. Therefore the long-term effect of such products cannot be scientifically evaluated. See **Holistic feeding stuffs and supplements**.

Aggravation Worsening of symptoms, usually associated with (in homoeopathy) administration of the correct remedy at an incorrect potency.

Agropyron repens see **Couch grass**.

Agrostemma githago see **Corn cockle**.

Alcohol In the form of spirits such as brandy, whisky, etc., alcohol was formerly used as a stimulant to increase the contractions of the heart by both number and force. Alcohol also has the effect of reducing body temperature. In some circumstances it could be used during fever to steady the pulse and respiration.

Alder buckthorn *(Frangula alnus)* A deciduous shrub measuring 4—5m. high. Although preferring damp, peaty soils and being found in many parts of Great Britain, it is absent from Scotland. Buckthorn is used medicinally as a laxative. It contains glycosides and is listed as a poison.

Alexander Technique A posture therapy developed by F.M.Alexander (1869—1955). While it has only recently gained popularity amongst riders, it has been continually practised by other adherents since around the year 1900. In recent years, many riders have found it beneficial both for themselves and for their horses. As applied to equitation, the technique is centred around helping the rider to realise the effects that bad posture and carriage have on the mind and body. Once these have been highlighted, the therapist seeks to change the rider's posture by gently moving the body into the correct position. Through improved co-ordination, the riding technique is greatly improved and the horse can become more supple, thereby avoiding musculo-skeletal problems such as back pain.

When used as part of a holistic approach, the Alexander Technique is an effective therapy. It is not a system of medicine in its own right. See **Posture**.

Alfalfa *(Medicago sativa)* Also known as lucerne, this crop has long been valued as a forage feed for horses. Although cultivated worldwide, it has only recently gained popularity in Great Britain. It is included in many commercially produced coarse mixes, being rich in minerals and vitamins.

Most of the lucerne produced in Britain is grown in East Anglia, and it is flash-dried which maximises retention of its nutritional content. Until recently, the processing of lucerne included the use of relatively high quantities of molasses, which is not desirable in equine feeds. However, some is now available with reduced, but still significant, amounts of sugar – see **Holistic feeding stuffs and supplements**.

Alium cepa see **Onion**.

Alkaloid A nitrogen-containing substance found in many plant species. Alkaloids affect bodily functions and are the basis for many modern drugs such as morphine, quinine, atrophine and codeine. Many narcotic drugs are composed of alkaloids: apart from the commonly known ones, such as marijuana from the hemp plant and opium from the poppy, they occur in many other plant materials. Nutmeg, for example, contains a powerful narcotic called myristicin.

Allergy A condition which arises when the body becomes hypersensitive to a particular substance. The nature of the condition depends upon the tissues affected, and either a local or general reaction can take place. Respiratory allergies, involving symptoms of varying severity, may be caused by agents such as hay dust and are associated with COPD. They may also arise from exposure to pollens during the summer months, when they may be associated with head-shaking. Other allergies, for example those associated with certain ingredients in feedstuffs, may cause a variety of symptoms such as skin problems and gastroenteritis.

Allergies arise from impaired immune function and can usually be remedied by natural medicines. Caution should be applied when vaccinating horses known to exhibit allergic responses.

Allium sativum see **Garlic**.

Allopathy A system of medicine utilizing agents to treat disease which are totally unrelated to the disease in their action. An example is antibiotics, which target bacteria, not the underlying disease.

Aloe *(Aloe vera)* A traditional purgative used for the treatment of constipation and colic. The genus *aloe* is mainly South African and includes trees and shrubs. *Aloe vera* is a particularly valuable healing agent when applied as a gell to burns, cuts and wounds. It has recently gained popularity as a general tonic and panacea – see **Panacea**.

Alterative A term used to describe a substance which improves health by gradually detoxifying the body and improving nutrition. The term 'blood cleanser' has largely replaced the word in recent times, but this can be a misleading expression. Strictly speaking, it is a remedy which alters the process of metabolism so that the tissues can deal more efficiently with nutrition and elimination of waste materials.

Alternative medicine Any systems of medicine or individual therapies which are unlike those employed by the conventional medical establishment of the day. (The phrase should properly be reserved for those systems of medicine able to substitute fully for conventional medicine – for example, it would not be a suitable description of physiotherapy.) In general, alternative therapies are aimed at returning the body to a healthy equilibrium, sometimes by using methods which may not be fully appreciated through contemporary scientific study. Such therapies concentrate as much on the underlying cause of the problem as on the disease itself. This approach is in contrast to modern conventional medicine (or, to give it a more appropriate term, 'technological medicine'), which tends to concentrate on relieving the symptoms of disease through the use of synthetic drug therapy.

Althaea officinalis

There is often confusion between the use of the word 'alternative' and the word 'complementary'. Compare **Complementary medicine**; see also **Holistic therapy, Traditional medicine**.

Althaea officinalis see **Marsh mallow**.

Alum The traditional term for sulphate of ammonia and alumina. Used mainly for its astringent properties, on wounds, ulcers, cracked heels, etc. Also used internally to check certain forms of diarrhoea.

Amino acid Amino acids are the fundamental constituents of all proteins. Some can be synthesised by the body itself; others, known as the 'essential amino acids', must be obtained from the diet.

Ammonia A colourless gas with a pungent odour, which can readily be compressed into a liquid. Traditionally used as an inhalant to stimulate the heart and thus quicken the pulse. Also used to stimulate the stomach and bowels. See **Sal volatile**.

Amylase An enzyme, present in the saliva and pancreatic juice, which breaks down starch in food.

Anaemia A lack of the oxygen-carrying red blood corpuscles, or haemoglobin. Symptoms of the condition include excessive tiredness, breathlessness during exercise and poor resistance to infection.

Anaerobe An organism that is unable to live in the absence of free oxygen. Compare **Aerobe**.

Anaesthetic A substance that deadens sensation and reduces pain.

Analgesic A drug that relieves pain. Many modern analgesics are based on traditional plant remedies, for example aspirin, is based on the chemical salicin from the willow tree, and morphine, is derived from the poppy. All pain-relievers depress vital functions and almost all are dangerous in quantity. Many poly-herbal feed additives contain analgesics such as Devil's claw *(Harpagophytum procumbens)*, which ideally should not be used on a regular basis without veterinary advice.

Anaphrodisiac   A substance which diminises sexual desire.

Anaphylaxis   Unusual, very sudden allergic reaction.

Anatomy   The study of the internal and external form and structure of living organisms. See also **Physiology**.

Angostura   A town which gave its name to an aromatic bitter obtained from the bark of the tree *Rutacea Cusparia*, which was traditionally used as a digestive stimulant.

Anise *(Pimpinella anisum)*   A plant which grows in Turkey and certain other countries. It is a valuable digestive aid and is useful in the treatment of respiratory problems. When given with ginger it is effective in assisting the expulsion of gas from the stomach and bowels. The parts of the plant normally used are the seeds.

Anodyne   Pain-relieving.

Antacid   A substance which reduces acid (especially in the stomach).

Anthelmintic   A substance which destroys parasitic worms and/or removes them from the body. Some traditional herbal anthelmintics are not available on general sale as they are potentially dangerous. Modern chemical wormers available through licensed retailers are effective but have the potential for harm to more sensitive animals. There are also increasing problems with certain worms being resistant, or developing resistance to, certain wormers, so it may be better to test dung samples regularly than to use wormers absolutely routinely when they may not be necessary. See also **Vermifuge**.

Anti-allergic A term used (especially in herbal medicine) to describe a substance which reduces the effects of allergic reaction.

Anti-anaemic A term used (especially in herbal medicine) to describe a substance which treats anaemia.

Antibacterial A substance which destroys or stops bacterial infections.

Antibiotic An anti-microbial therapeutic agent originally synthesised by living organisms (e.g. fungi). Originally, the modern antibiotics were highly effective, but they were used only when all else had failed. Gradually, they have become over-used and many strains of bacteria have developed immunity to them, and therefore resist treatment with such products. There is also a phenomenon of transfer of resistance from one bacterium to another, or even between different species of bacteria. Compare **Anti-infective**.

Antibody Antibodies build onto and neutralise hostile substances within the body, thus protecting it from infection and disease. The immune system, which is responsible for their formation, will also try to reject any other foreign substancesfrom the body.

Anti-emetic A substance which relieves nausea and vomiting.

Anti-fungal A substance which treats fungal infections. There are many preparations available, both herbal and pharmaceutical. Garlic *(Allium sativum)* is an example of a natural fungicide.

Anti-haemorrhagic   A term used (especially in herbal medicine) to describe a substance which stops bleeding and haemorrhage.

Anti-histamine   In herbal medicine, the term is used to describe a substance which neutralises the effects of histamine in an allergic response. In modern medicine the word is used to describe a drug which inhibits the production of histamine.

Anti-hydrolic   A substance which reduces or suppresses perspiration.

Anti-infective   A term used to describe herbal remedies which may be used to help resist infection. They work by strengthening the body's own defences, rather than by attacking specific organisms. Compare **Antibiotic**.

Anti-inflammatory   A substance which reduces inflammation. Modern drugs which suppress the inflammatory process are not without the risk of side-effects and inevitably counteract the healing process. The majority of herbal anti-inflammatories act by eliminative circulatory or metabolic action; some contain constituents which are chemically close to steroid drugs. One, Devil's claw *(Harpagophytum procumbens)*, is commonly found in poly-herbal feed supplements; its use may contravene the rules of competition sport.

Antilithic   A substance which dissolves stones or gravel in the kidneys or bladder

Anti-microbial   A substance which destroys or inhibits the growth of micro-organisms.

Antimony   A brittle, blueish white element of metallic appearance. Traditionally used to improve the coat and skin and also to slow the circulation of the blood. Also used as a sudorific (to induce sweating).

Anti-mucous A term used (especially in herbal medicine) to describe a substance which reduces mucus.

Antineoplastic A term used (especially in herbal medicine) to describe a substance which has anti-cancer properties.

Antiopathy A system of medicine using agents to suppress disease symptoms. Many modern drugs fall into this category.

Antioxidant A substance used to prevent oxidisation of foodstuffs. Many manufactured feeds contain chemical antioxidants of unknown effect on the horse's bowel flora. The health implications of some of these chemicals are also unknown.

Antiperiodic A term formerly used to describe substances which prevent recurrence of diseases whose nature it is to return periodically.

Anti-pruritic A term used to describe an agent which relieves itching (pruritis).

Anti-pyretic reduces fever by lowering the body temperature. See **Febrifuge**.

Anti-rheumatic A substance which relieves rheumatism and arthritis.

Antiseptic A substance which destroys or inhibits the growth of disease-causing bacteria and other micro-organisms. Antiseptics are usually antagonistic to pathogenic organisms on contact. Many herbs, such as arbor-vitae, marigold and thyme, contain substances which are antiseptic and may be used as the basis for topical wound washes.

Antispasmodic A substance which relieves spasms or cramps. There are various natural antispasmodics, such as mint *(Mentha piperita / spicata)*, which are suitable for equine use.

Anti-thrombotic A substance which prevents blood clots.

Anti-toxic A substance which clears toxins from the system.

Antitussive A substance which relieves coughing

Anti-viral A substance which destroys or stops viral infections.

Anus The opening at the end of the alimentary canal, through which waste material (faeces) is discharged.

Aperient A mild laxative which helps to gently stimulate the natural actions of the bowel, rather than provoke them.

Apple cider vinegar A form of vinegar which has gained a wide reputation amongst horse owners as a preventative of arthritic disorders and many other chronic complaints. It is claimed to normalise digestive secretions and to improve calcium metabolism.

Aquilegia vulgaris see **Columbine**.

Arctium lappa see **Burdock, greater**.

Armoracia rusticana *see* **Horseradish**.

Aristolochia clematis see **Birthwort**.

Arnica (*Arnica montana*) Also known as wolf's bane and leopard's bane. A herb common in central Europe, found on poor grassland and heaths, and commonly used in herbal medicine and homoeopathy. It is used for the treatment of wounds, bruises, and many other kinds of injury. It is toxic when taken internally except in homoeopathic doses, which are extremely dilute.

Aromatherapy The therapeutic use of essences or oils,

either massaged into the skin or administered through the olfactory system. On occasion, they are also given orally. The origins of aromatherapy can be traced back to the early Egyptians, who administered some of their plant medicines in this way. Essential oils can be used in the treatment of a variety of ailments, providing anti-bacterial, bactericidal, anti-viral and anti-inflammatory actions. They may also be used to affect the horse's mental state.

When properly used as part of a holistic approach to medicine, aromatherapy can be very effective. It is not a system of medicine in its own right, although some agents are extremely powerful pharmacologically.

Arsenate of iron A chemical preparation formerly used as a tonic and restorative for horses in low condition. Also used in the treatment of some forms of skin diseases.

Arsenic Occurs in nature as a free metal, and also in combination with other metals. It can be used medicinally, but excessive intakes of arsenic are highly oxic. Traditionally it was used internally as an alterative, and as a stomachic (stimulant to the stomach) to aid digestion. It was also used in paste form to destroy warts and other growths, as a fumigant in the treatment of glanders and, in solution, to kill parasites. When used by unskilled horsemen as a wormer it sometimes had fatal results. See also **Orpiment**.

Arsenious oxide A chemical preparation formerly used as a tonic, astringent and alterative. Given for indigestion, general debility, and used for the treatment of skin diseases such as eczema and psoriasis. Most commonly given in the form of *Liquor arsenicalis*.

Artery A blood vessel conveying blood away from the heart at high pressure.

Arthritis Inflammation of a joint, usually involving pain, stiffness, swelling, heat, and restriction of movement.

Artemisia arbrotanum see **Southernwood**.

Artemisia absinthium see **Wormwood**.

Asafoetida *(Ferula asa-foetida)* A foul-smelling medicinal gum resin from the roots and rhizomes of a herb which grows mainly in Afghanistan and Iran. It is used in the treatment of chronic bronchitis and for its calming effect on the gut. It is also known as devil's dung.

Ascarid Any nematode worm of the parasitic genus *Ascaris* infecting the small intestines. See also **Anthelmintic**.

Ascites Fluid accumulation in the abdominal cavity.

Ascorbic Acid Vitamin C, see **Vitamins**.

Aspergillus A type of fungus which thrives in dusty hay and straw. It is associated with respiratory problems in horses, such as COPD.

Astringent A substance which contracts tissue, thereby reducing secretions or discharges. Notable natural astringents include oak bark *(Quercus robur)* and catechu, which is an extract of various plants from India such as betel-nut, acacia etc.

Ataxia Loss of muscular co-ordination.

Atrophy The wasting away of a normally developed organ or tissue. It can be caused by undernourishment, disuse, or ageing.

Auscultation Examination of a patient by listening (with or without a stethoscope).

Avoirdupois A system of weights in which a pound is equal to sixteen ounces.

Azoturia A condition otherwise known as Monday morning disease, 'tying up' or 'set-fast'. Specific cases may also be referred to as myoglobinuria or exertional rhabdomyolysis. The horse develops swelling and pain in the muscles of the loins and hindquarters, and sweats profusely. In severe cases the horse will be unable to move. The condition is associated with performance animals who are kept on full rations whilst stabled. Holistic therapy in general has achieved success in treatment; provision of holistic nutrition is important in prevention.

Bach, Dr Edward The founder of Bach's Flower Remedies. He was a qualified medical doctor who developed a system of treatment using the stored energy from plants. Many different remedies are available and the choice depends on the emotional state of the patient. Flower remedies can be used very successfully in equine medicine when properly integrated with other holistic therapies. However, as with many holistic therapies, success depends a great deal on the expertise of the practitioner.

Bach was also associated with homoeopathy and the development of bowel nosodes.

Bacteraemia Presence of bacteria in the bloodstream.

Bacteria A group of mainly uni-cellular micro-organisms, which are associated with many diseases. Bacteria live in soil, water, or air, or as parasites of man, animals and plants. Most multiply asexually by simple division. Compare **Virus**.

Bactericidal Describes substances capable of destroying bacteria, including antibiotics, antiseptics and disinfectants.

Bael fruit The fruit of an thorny Indian tree *(Aegle marmelos)*. Traditionally used in combination with alkalis and aromatics to arrest diarrhoea in foals.

BAHNM see **British Association of Holistic Nutrition and Medicine**.

Balling gun A device which works on the principle of a child's pop gun, used to administer medicinal balls.

Balling iron Another name for a gag, used to hold the horse's mouth open for the administration of medicinal balls. This method of giving medicines has fallen into disuse: it was not particularly effective, because of the difficulty that a horse has in swallowing with his mouth open. However, balling irons were used successfully during other procedures which required the mouth to be kept open. See **Balling gun**, **Horse balls**.

Balsams Aromatic fluids of plant origin, originally those taken from the *Balsaminaceae* family. Other balsams include those of Peru *(Myroxylon Pereirae)* and Tolu *(Myroxylon toluifera)*. The formulation Friar's balsam is well known. Traditional uses of balsams included skin preparations, mild antiseptics, and inhalations for respiratory problems.The inhalants were commonly prepared by mixing them with hot water and bran, the vapour being administered via a nosebag.

Barley *(Hordeum vulgare* and other species) A hardy species of grass, producing grains which may be used to provide energy in a horse's ration. Barley contains a higher level of starch than oats, and is known as a fattening feed. Most horses with good teeth can cope with uncooked whole grains, but it is probably best to feed them either crimped or cooked so that the nutrients are more readily available. Steam cooking is preferable to either micronisation or extrusion.

Bay *(Laurus nobilis)* Also known as sweet bay and bay laurel. An evergreen shrub which comes from Mediterranean coasts. Cultivated as an ornamental plant in some areas, notably the south-west of England and Ireland. Traditionally, bay leaves were used as an ingredient in fomentations. The berries were used as a stomachic, and were an ingredient of the ancient stomachic powder known as diapente (a medicine of five ingredients).

Beans Leguminous plants, the seeds of which are used as a source of energy. Field beans are frequently incorporated into coarse mixes. They contain 23—27% protein and are a valuable source of lysine.

Beef peptone A protein-like material derived from beef and unwisely used as an ingredient in some supplements for horses.

Beef tea A broth made by boiling beef bones from which the majority of the meat had been removed. Formerly used as a tonic for invalid horses.

Behavioural problems Equine activities which are unacceptable to the owner. These can take many forms and may arise for a variety of reasons including training, riding technique, saddle-fitting problems, environmental factors, and diet. Many behavioural problems are associated with the use of molasses in feedstuffs, or with the improper use of grains, which causes the horse to become hyperactive. See **Holistic feeding stuffs and supplements**, **Stress**.

 Belladonna *(Atropa belladonna)* Also known as deadly nightshade. A herb found on waste and stony ground in central Europe and southern Britain. The plant is rich in alkaloids and is used in herbal medicine to reduce spasm in the gut wall and urinary tract. It can also be used to reduce salivation and perspiration. A few drops of juice in the eye dilates the pupil, which facilitates eye examination. Interestingly, Renaissance ladies were in the habit of using it to produce the same effect and thus make their eyes more attractive, hence the name (Italian: beautiful woman).

Belladonna is extremely toxic, and can be deadly if used incorrectly. In homoeopathic medicine it is safe and can prove very effective. It is listed as a poison.

Bellis perennis see **Daisy**.

Benign A term used to describe a condition or disorder which does not produce harmful effects; often used to describe a tumour that is not cancerous. Compare **Malignant**.

Benzoin Also known as Gum Benjamin. The aromatic, resinous juice of *Styrax benzoin*, a tree found in Java and Sumatra. Used in Friar's Balsam. See **Balsam**, **Styrax**.

Beta tocopherol Vitamin E, see **Vitamins.**

Bezoar stone A stony substance found in the stomachs of some animals such as goats, antelopes and llamas. Formerly esteemed as the antidote to all poisons, and used in many ancient remedies.

 Bicarbonate of potash A chemical preparation formerly used in the treatment of rheumatism and, when combined with vegetable bitters, for digestive problems. Also used externally to suppress itching, and as a cleanser.

Bile A green, alkaline liquid, which is manufactured by the liver and trickles continuously into the duodenum as part of the digestive process.

Bio- Prefix denoting life or living organisms, as in 'biological'.

Bio-availability Commonly refers to the degree to which a nutrient becomes available to the body after ingestion. Processing and refining of ingredients can alter digestibility and absorbtion, thus affecting nutrient bio-availability. Artificial additives to horse feeds, such as synthetic vitamins, are thought to have poor bio-availability.

Bioflavonoids see **Flavonoids**.

Biotin A vitamin of the B complex. See **Vitamins**.

Birthwort *(Aristolochia clematitis)* A plant common in the wine-growing areas of central Europe. It also grows around the Mediterranean, in Turkey and the Caucasus. It has been introduced to Britain, but is rare and scattered. It was formerly used to treat infections. The roots, considered to be one of the strongest plant astringents, were used to stop haemorrhaging, being administered either as a powder or, when boiled in water, as a drench.

Bishoping   A method of altering the appearance of the horse's teeth by filing them and burning them with a hot iron. Formerly used to give a false impression of age by recreating the black marks which exist in the teeth of younger animals, but which wear away as the horse gets older.

Bismuth   A brittle reddish-white element. Traditionally used as an astringent, in the form of a powder or solution, and for the treatment of diarrhoea.

Bistort see **Snakeroot.**

Bitters   The term used to describe a group of herbs which share the same, or similar, chemical characteristics and which are usually bitter in taste. Bitter herbs are commonly used for the treatment of digestive disorders and to stimulate the appetite.

Bittersweet *(Solanum dulcamara)*   Also known as woody nightshade. A plant common in Europe and much of Asia, growing in wet woodland, banks, clearings, marsh and fen. Traditionally used as a narcotic and diuretic. While the plant is a valuable homoeopathic remedy it is toxic in its undiluted form, and is dangerous in the wrong hands.

Blackberry *(Rubus fruticosis)*   A common rambling shrub found in hedgerows and waste places around the world. The leaves are astringent and healing, being rich in tannins and flavonoids.

Black box see **Radionics**.

Black bryony see **Bryony, black**.

Black nightshade *(Solanum nigrum)* Also known as garden nightshade. An erect, branched annual (occasionally biennial) plant measuring from below 10cm up to 60cm in height. A highly successful and troublesome weed in cultivated land. The plant contains toxic alkaloids and is listed as a poison — see **Poisonous plants**.

Blacksmith see **Farrier**.

Bladderwrack A common brown seaweed with air-filled bladders.

Bleeders A term commonly used to describe horses who discharge blood from their nostrils during and/or immediately after hard exercise. The condition, also known as epistaxis, is associated with bleeding from the dorsal areas of the lungs.

Bleeding Removal of blood from the body. Bleeding was formerly used in the treatment of ailments such as laminitis and many other conditions where it was thought that benefit would be derived from the operation. It was considered safe to withdraw as much as a gallon of blood from a horse, every month for several months in succession. The let blood was collected for inspection in order that its general condition, colour, etc. could be taken into consideration when making a diagnosis.

Bleeding was often carried out indiscriminately by the uninitiated and blood was sometimes let in sufficiently large quantities to seriously weaken or even kill the animal.

There are some acupuncture techniques which safely apply the art of bleeding.

Blepharospasm Spasm of the eyelids.

Blister beetle see **Cantharides**, **Blistering and rowelling**.

Blistering and rowelling   The process of blistering involved artificially inducing inflammation of the skin, commonly by the application of iodide of mercury, or the dried and powdered bodies of the Spanish fly or blister-beetle (cantharides). Rowelling involved the introduction of some material such as tow or a piece of old leather under the surface of the skin for the same or a similar purpose: the skin was separated from the flesh beneath to form a 'pocket' to receive the material to which the blistering agent had previously been applied.

Traditionally, blistering and rowelling were commonly used in the treatment of fractures, dislocations, joint problems, and other conditions where it was felt that an accumulation of body fluids at, or near, the site of the injury would facilitate the healing process. In the case of rowelling, body fluids would ooze from the wound as it was kept open by the application of products such as savine (an irritant, volatile oil of juniper).

There were other theories as to why this ancient practice might be beneficial, one being 'counter-irritation', whereby the existing trauma was supposed to have been diverted to the new site of irritation.

Blistering was also used by some horsemen in an attempt to cure a hard mouth; in fact it had the opposite effect, as although the mouth was temporarily sensitised by the process, hardened and less sensitive skin eventually grew over the site of the injury. See also **Firing**, **Savine**, **Seton**.

Blood pressure   The pressure of the blood against the walls of the main arteries, which varies with age and physical condition.

Blue vitriol   Hydrated copper sulphate — see **Sulphate of copper**.

Bogbean *(Menyanthes trifoliata)*   Semi-aquatic hairless perennial plant preferring marshy places. Found in Europe, Asia and North America. Traditionally used as a digestive stimulant

Bog spavin see **Spavin**.

Bole A bright red earthy clay formerly used in astringent remedies and as a base to give constistency to ointments.

Bone Hard connective tissue that forms the skeleton of the body.

Bone marrow see **Marrow**.

Bone spavin see **Spavin**.

Borax Sodium borate, deposited by evaporation of alkaline lakes. A mild disinfectant used in the treatment of skin diseases, and also for mouth washes.

Borderline nutrition A situation that is created by choosing inappropriate raw materials for feedstuffs and supplements. The effects may be seen in animals fed on diets formulated principally on cost and inappropriate scientific assessment, rather than their suitability for the evolved reqirements of the species. It may also be seen in animals kept on florally depleted pasture (or on forage made from such pasture). Although such animals can appear to be in good health and condition, they may have reduced reserves of vitality, which may compromise their ability to overcome unusual physiological stresses. In such circumstances borderline nutrition may be a predisposing factor in either sub-clinical or clinical disease, just as would be the case with outright nutritional imbalances or deficiencies. See **Holistic feeding stuffs and supplements**, **Inverted nutrition**.

Boric acid A chemical preparation formerly used as an antiseptic. 'Antiseptic cotton wool' was prepared by soaking cotton wool in a solution of boric acid, and then drying for future use.

Bot-fly The name for various flies of the family *Oestridae* which lay their eggs on horses — see **Gadfly**.

Bots (Gastrophilus spp.) The maggot of a bot-fly. This lays its eggs on the hairs of the horse's shoulders, legs and neck during the summer months. When the horse licks itself, it takes the eggs into the mouth; when the eggs hatch the larvae lodge in the stomach and other sites, where they live as parasites. When they are mature, some 8—10 months later, they pass out of the horse in the droppings and eventually hatch as adult flies to complete the cycle. See **Anthelmintic**.

Bracken *(Pteridium aquilinum)* A fern plant measuring up to 2m high, common in woodland areas of Great Britain. Bracken is toxic and also contains a substance which is antagonistic to thiamine (Vitamin B1). It is a common cause of serious or fatal poisoning in horses, and is listed as a poison — see **Poisonous plants**.

Bran The fibrous husks which cover grain seed. Traditionally the chief use for bran was as a mild laxative, given as a 'bran mash', perhaps once a week. This counteracted the possible constipatory effects of large proportions of hard feed in the diet of horses in hard work. The use of bran has fallen out of favour for a variety of reasons, but largely because most people do not feed straights nowadays. Modern bran is inferior to traditional bran and should be fed with care to avoid nutritional imbalances. Bran can be a good food if the calcium levels are balanced in the whole diet,

Bran poultice A traditional dressing to 'draw' wounds. Bran and crushed linseed were often mixed together in equal parts for this purpose.

Brassicas Members of the cabbage family. Certain members, such as kale and turnip, can deplete the body of iodine and can cause anaemia.

Brewers grains   A by-product of the brewing industry. Dried brewers grains are obtained by drying residues of malted and unmalted cereals and other starchy matter.

British Association of Holistic Nutrition and Medicine (BAHNM)   The BAHNM operates in five main areas:
1)   Dissemination of technical material on holistic management, nutrition and medicine.
2)   Administration of a licensing procedure for holistic products manufactured to a recognised Quality Standard.
3)   Operation of a referral system for horse owners wishing to obtain the services of properly qualified and experienced practioners of holistic therapies.
4)   Collaboration with government departments involved with relevant legislation, such as the *Feeding Stuffs Regulations*, the *Medicines Act* and the *Trade Descriptions Act*. See page **13** for contact details.
5)   Advice and guidance on holistic equine management.
See also **Holism, Holistic feeding stuffs and supplements, Holistic saddles and registered holistic saddle fitters**.

British Association of Homoeopathic Veterinary Surgeons (BAHVS)   The BAHVS is an association formed to promote education and research into veterinary homoeopathy, together with its practice. It holds seminars, publishes a newsletter and provides names of veterinarians practising homoeopathy to enquirers. The BAHVS also runs post-graduate courses and examinations for veterinary surgeons practising homoeopathy. Those qualifying may use the letters Vet.F.F.Hom. after their name. See page **13** for contact details. See also **Homoeopathy**.

Broken wind see **Small airway disease.**

Bromide of potassium   A chemical preparation formerly

used as a sedative, having a powerful action on the nervous system.

Bronch- Prefix meaning relating to the bronchial tree.

Bronchial tree A branching system of tubes which conducts air to the lungs. Includes the bronchi and bronchioles.

Bronchitis Inflammation of the bronchi — see **Bronchial tree**.

I ▶ **Broom** *(Sarothamnus scoparius)* A shrub which is common in dry, hilly areas throughout Britain, western Europe and Scandinavia. Used in herbal medicine, it has cardioactive and diuretic properties, and should only be used by appropriately qualified and experienced practitioners. It is also used in homoeopathy for cardiac problems. Broom tops are a traditional anthelmintic. Broom is listed as poisonous — see **Poisonous plants**.

Bruise An injury to the skin and underlying tissue. The asociated discolouration is caused by the escape of blood from the ruptured vessels.

Bryonia dioica see **Bryony, white**.

I ▶ **Bryony, black** *(Tamus communis)* A climbing plant found in scrub, hedgerows, and wood margins. Common throughout southern England, the Midlands and Wales. Although it is listed as poisonous plant, little is known about its poisonous principle, which is sometimes stated to be a glycoside. See **Poisonous plants.**

I ▶ **Bryony, white** *(Bryonia dioica)* A climbing plant which grows in hedges, in wet woodland and woodland edges, on waste ground and up fences. Found in western and central Europe, it is common in lowland England, but not native to Scotland or Ireland. It was formerly used by unscrupulous horse dealers to promote short-term condition, which soon disappeared, leaving the animal seriously debilitated. It is used in herbal medicine for its purgative, expectorant, vermifuge and diaphoretic properties, and is also used in homoeopathic remedies. It is listed as a poisonous plant — see **Poisonous plants.**

Buckthorn *(Rhamnus cathartica)*   A thorny deciduous shrub reaching 4—6m in height; prefers calcareous soils and is a native of Britain. It can be used medicinally as a laxative, hence its alternative name; Purging Buckthorn. Syrup of Buckthorn is listed as a poison — see **Poisonous plants**.

Buckwheat *(Fagopyrum esculentum)*   An erect annual plant native to central Asia and cultivated elsewhere. Buckwheat contains the flavonoid glycoside, rutin, and is used medicinally in the treatment of circulatory disorders, and also as an antihistamine.

Bulling   see **Grunting**.

Burdock, greater *(Arctium lappa)*   A robust plant which grows on footpaths, waste ground, river banks, in scrub and in wood clearings. It is found throughout most of Europe and is common in the British Isles. Burdock was formerly used as an ingredient for an ointment known as pompillion, used by blacksmiths, and also as an ingredient for infusions to make a tonic. It is a valuable homoeopathic remedy for skin problems. Burdock should not be given to pregnant mares.

Burgundy pitch   A resin made by preparing and straining the exudation of a species of fir tree (Norway spruce). Formerly used to strengthen plasters and in some ointments.

Burnet, greater *(Sanguisorba officianalis)*   A perennial herb common in England, Europe and North America. In herbal medicine it is used as an astringent. It is recommended for horse pastures — see **Meadow**.

Burnett's Disinfecting Fluid   A traditional proprietary disinfectant fluid containing chloride of zinc.

Bute see **Phenylbutazone**.

By-products   A term used in the animal food industry to describe a substance which is a waste product from another industry. For example 'wheat feed' is a by-product of flour manufacture, consisting principally of fragments of the outer skins and screened particles of grain. There are about 140 by-products available to the animal feed industry from around the world. Some are included in inferior horse feeds, mainly on the basis of cost. Most by-products have been de-natured and are lacking in holistic nutrients. See **Fortification**; compare **Holistic feedingstuffs and supplements**.

Cadmium   A white toxic metal occurring in zinc ores. It has caused poisoning in horses grazing near zinc smelters.

Caffeine   An alkaloid drug present in coffee and tea. It has a stimulating effect on the nervous system and is also a diuretic.

I ▶ Calabar bean   The seed of a tropical African plant *(Physostigma venenosa)* which has powerful sedative properties. Traditionally used in horses to control spasms of tetanus; also used in ophthalmic procedures, where it has the affect of dilating the pupil.

Calciferol   Vitamin D – see **Vitamins**.

Calcification   The deposit of calcium salts in tissue. This occurs as a normal part of bone formation.

Calcified seaweed   A species of seaweed *(Lithothamnium calcareum)* which grows into a hard, coral-like stucture. See **Kelp**.

Calcium A major mineral available in the horse's natural diet, quantities varying amongst individual foods. An important constituent of bones, teeth and blood. Also important in nerve function, muscle contraction and blood clotting. See **Mineral**.

Calendula officinalis see **Marigold**.

Calorie A term used to indicate the energy value of foods, now largely superseded by the joule (1 calorie = 4.1855 joules).

Calumba The root of an east African plant *(Jateorhiza palmata)*. One of the most valuable bitter tonics, also having a carminative action on the gut. Traditionally used with nux vomica and mineral acids in the form of an infusion, and with bicarbonate of soda to treat acidic forms of stomach trouble.

Camphor A volatile oil obtained from the camphor tree. Traditionally used as a stimulant to the skin, and as an ingredient of linaments used for sprains and muscle and joint stiffness. Also used internally as a stomach stimulant and anti-spasmodic, and for some forms of colic and diarrhoea. In common with many strong-smelling substances, camphor is damaging to homoeopathic remedies.

Cancer A malignant growth which invades adjacent tissue and spreads to other parts of the body, often remote from the original site. It is estimated that many thousands of potentially malignant cells are sucessfully eliminated every day by the body's formidable defence systems. Holistic medicine is less concerned with attacking the specific tumour than with developing an overall strategy which will strengthen the body's own powers to overcome the problem.

Canella A genus of aromatic trees, the bark of which yields a digestive stimulant; otherwise known as white cinammon or canella bark.

Canker A chronic disease affecting the tissues of the foot, causing damaged and softened hoof tissue. Characterised by a foul-smelling discharge.

Cannabis sativa see **Indian hemp**.

Cantharides *(Lytta vesicatoria)* Otherwise known as 'Spanish fly' or 'blister beetle', from which is prepared the toxic and irritant chemical compound cantharidin. Apart from its traditional external application in blistering and rowelling, cantharides was also used internally as an irritant in some cases of digestive problems. See also **Blistering and rowelling**.

Capillary An extremely narrow blood vessel. Capillaries form networks in most tissues for the distribution of blood. Their walls are thin enough to allow the exchange of oxygen, carbon dioxide, salts and water between the blood and the tissues.

Capped hock, elbow and knee Injuries which result from mechanical damage to the affected joint. Capped hock and elbow involve swellings filled with synovial fluid, which is the lubricating fluid of the joint. These swellings normally reduce of their own accord, the synovial fluid being re-absorbed into the body. A capped knee tends to become hard and calloused rather than fluid-filled.

Capsicum A tropical shrub of the potato family yielding cayenne pepper. Traditionally used as a carminative for digestive problems. See also **Pimento**.

Caraway *(Carum carvi)* A biennial plant common in moist meadows in Europe and central Asia. The seeds contain the essential oil, carvon, traditionally used in the treatment of colic and for bronchial conditions.

Carbohydrate Any one of a large of group of compounds including cellulose, sugars and starch. Manufactured by plants, carbohydrates contain the energy that the body requires for cell processes and physical function. They provide energy for muscle contraction and are therefore important in the diet of performance horses. If fed in a greater quantity than can be utilised they are stored by the body as fat.

Carbolic acid see **Phenol**.

Carbonate of ammonia A chemical preparation formerly used with vegetable bitters as a stimulant in the treatment of specific fevers. Also used as an expectorant and for the relief of indigestion, flatulence and colic.

Carbon dioxide A colourless gas formed in the body tissues during metabolism and carried in the blood to the lungs, where it is exhaled.

Carcinoma Cancer that arises in the epithelium, the tissue that lines the skin and internal organs.

Cardi- Prefix denoting the heart.

Cardiac Of, relating to, or affecting the heart.

Cardioactive The term used for a substance that has a noticable influence on heart function. For example, in herbal medicine, the foxglove *(Digitalis purpurea / lanata)*.

Cardiovascular system The heart, together with the network of vessels which circulate blood around the body.

Cardamom A spice made from the seeds of *Elittaria cardomomum,* a tropical plant of the ginger family. Traditionally used for its carminative action on the stomach.

Carminative A term used (epecially in herbal medicine) to describe a substance which eases cramping pains and expels flatulence. The principal action is a soothing, settling effect on the gut wall.

Carotenoids Any of a number of reddish-yellow pigments widely distributed in plants.The carotenoid, carotene, is a source of vitamin A.

Carron oil A traditional remedy for scalds and burns, consisting of equal parts of lime water and linseed oil.

Carrot The tapering root of a plant of the *Umbelliferae* family. A nutritious vegetable which can be used to vary the horse's diet from time to time. Carrots should be carefully sliced so that the horse has to chew them. Small, irregular shaped pieces can escape the teeth and have the potential to choke the animal. Pulped carrots were traditionally given as a treatment for worms. Some horses are especially sensitive to the agricultural sprays used on many carrot crops.

Cartilage Dense connective tissue consisting mainly of chondroitin sulphate and capable of withstanding high pressure.

Carum carvi see **Caraway**.

Cascarilla An extract of the bark of an Indian tree *(Croton eleuteria)* traditionally used as a bitter tonic in the treatment of digestive disorders.

Cast 1)A horse is said to be cast when he lies on the ground and is unable to rise without assistance This usually happens in the stable as a result of lack of room, or because his movement is blocked by an obstacle such as a wall.
2)Horses made to lie down and secured in that position for examination, or for an operation are also said to have been cast. See also **Side line**.

Castor oil An oil made from the seeds of a tropical African plant *(Ricinus communis)*. Traditionally used as a laxative.

Catechu *(Acacia catechu)* A powerful astringent extracted from the heartwood of a tree of the Acacia family. Traditionally used in the treatment of diarrhoea, gut infections and irritations. Also combined with opium and chalk to moderate and complement its actions.

Cat-gut see **Sutures**.

Catharsis Purging or cleansing out of the bowels by giving a laxative (cathartic) to stimulate intestinal activity

Caustic A substance that causes irritation and burning, and destroys tissue.

Cauterise To burn with a caustic agent or hot iron with the purpose of the destruction of morbid tissue, the arrest of haemorrhage, or castration.Mostly obsolete — see also **Firing**.

Celandine, Greater *(Chelidonium majus)*, Also known as Celandine poppy, Wart wort. An erect, branched plant which reaches 60cm in height, preferring banks and hedgerows, found in most parts of Britain except Scotland. Traditionally used externally in the treatment of warts and internally for liver, lung and gastro-intestinal problems; also for rheumatism Used in homoeopathy in diluted form. The celandine contains many potentially toxic alkaloids and is listed as a poison (see **Poisonous plants**), but it has an unpalatable taste and poisoning is comparatively rare.

Celery *(Apium graviolens)* A hairless, biennial plant up to 1m tall, common in Europe but rather local in the British Isles. Prefers ditches and wet areas. Widely cultivated for human consumption. Used medicinally for digestive problems, and also for rheumatism and arthritis. Because the wild plant can be toxic in some circumstances; cultivated forms are preferable.

Cell The basic unit of all living organisms, which can reproduce itself exactly.

Cell proliferator A term used (especially in herbal medicine) to describe a substance that enhances the formation of new tissue to speed the healing process.

Cellulose A carbohydrate forming the chief component of the cell walls of plants. It contributes to the strength of the structure, enabling grasses to stand upright. A large part of the horse's diet consists of cellulose.

Celsius see **Centigrade temperature**.

Centesimal Scale of dilution of a homoeopathic remedy, each stage being one in one hundred.

Centigrade temperature Temperature expressed on a scale in which the melting point of ice is assigned a value of 0 degrees, and the boiling point of water a value of 100 degrees. Constructed by a man named Celsius.

Central nervous system The brain and the spinal cord.

Cerate The name formerly given to ointments or salves in which wax was an prominent ingredient.

Chaff Traditionally, a horse's concentrate ration was bulked up with chaff, consisting of chopped hay and straw. This was done to encourage the horse to chew properly and to discourage bolting of feed. Modern chaffs are usually mixed with molasses, which should be avoided if possible as it affects digestion, amongst other things. Chaffs with reduced (but still significant) amounts of molasses are available, but it is better to use products which are free from molasses. See **Holistic feedingstuffs and supplements**, **BAHNM**.

Chalk   A soft, white rock composed of calcium carbonate. Traditionally used as an antacid in preparations for the treatment of diarrhoea; also to form a mechanical protective barrier for the mucous membrane of the intestines.

Chamberlie   A traditional term for human urine when used in remedies.

▶ **Chamomile** *(Chamaemelum nobile)*   A plant which grows in dry, sandy soil, often coastal; found in western Europe and in local areas of southern Britain and south-west Ireland. A valuable herb, used for its calming properties. It relaxes the viscera and is also a valuable bitter tonic, useful in remedies for digestive disorders. In addition it has anodyne properties and is a valuable homoeopathic remedy.

Charcoal   The carbonaceous residue of wood that has undergone smothered combustion. Traditionally used for wound dressings to absorb foul material and odour; usually mixed with bran and made into a poultice. Its use in the treatment of wounds, especially ulcers, is being revived.

Charges   see **Plasters**.

Chelidonium majus   see **Celandine, Greater**.

Chemotherapeutic   A chemical agent used in conventional medicine to combat bacterial or protozoal infection, for example antibiotic, sulphadimidine.

Chickweed *(Stellaria media)*   One of the commonest weeds with worldwide distribution, found in gardens, fields, on waste ground, etc. Chickweed is used in homoeopathy for the treatment of rheumatism, arthritis and bronchitis. The plant contains saponins and is listed as a poison, but it has only very rarely been associated with poisoning — see **Poisonous plants**.

Chicory *(Cichorium intybus)* A herb which grows at roadsides, in waste places, and on some pastures through most of Europe. Used in homoeopathy as an appetite stimulant, and to treat flatulance and stomach pains. Recommended for horse pastures — see **Meadow**.

Chiropractic A system of treating ailments by manipulation of the body using gentle, high-velocity, low-amplitude impulses. Chiropractic was founded in the United States by David Daniel Palmer (1845-1913). It is commonly used to treat horses. There is recognised training in animal chiropractic by the McTimoney school. Chiropractors must work under the direction of a veterinary surgeon.

Chloral hydrate A chemical preparation formerly used as an anaesthetic. It is used in modern human medicine as a sedative and hypnotic drug, mainly for children and the elderly.

Chlorate of potassium A chemical preparation formerly used internally for the treatment of fevers. Also used to treat ulceration of the mouth and throat. The preparation is used in laboratories as a source of oxygen and in the manufacture of matches, and it detonates on exposure to heat.

Chloric ether A chemical preparation formerly used as a stimulant, antispasmodic and anodyne. Popular for the treatment of colic, shocks and asthma — see also **Ether**.

Chloride of ammonium A chemical preparation formerly used internally in the treatment of bronchial catarrh, congestion of the liver and rheumatism. When dissolved in water with saltpetre, it was used to cool horses' legs.

Chloride of mercury (Mercuric chloride) A preparation formerly used internally as a purgative. Also used as an alterative in the treatment of chronic skin diseases and lymphangitis.

Chloride of zinc A caustic preparation formerly used for destroying warts and other growths on the skin. Also used as an antiseptic and disinfectant to assist in the healing of difficult wounds.

Chlorine A gaseous element which is closely associated with sodium and potassium, and which shares their role in the regulation of body fluids. 'Chlorine gas', a fumigant formerly used to disinfect stables, was produced by sprinkling chlorinated lime powder onto floor surfaces.

Chloroform A volatile liquid, formerly used as a general anaesthetic

Cholagogue A term used (especially in herbal medicine) to describe a substance that increases the flow of bile into the intestines.

Choline A basic compound often classified as a vitamin, which, strictly speaking, it is not. Choline is essential for building and maintaining cell structure, and is associated with fat metabolism and nerve function. Widely distributed in feedstuffs, it can also be synthesised by the body.

Chorea Rhythmic, uncontrolled movement of limbs or neck.

Chronic Describes a disease of gradual onset and long duration, usually involving slow changes. Compare **Acute**.

Cichorium intybus see **Chicory**.

Cicuta virosa see **Cowbane**.

Cider vinegar see **Apple cider vinegar**.

Cinchona *(Cinchona succirubra)* Also known as Jesuits' bark and Fever tree; the bark is the source of quinine. It has many uses in equine medicine; for the treatment of fever in general and as a bitter digestive tonic. Formerly used extensively with alcohol in the treatment of equine flu. See **Quinine**, **Homoeopathy**.

Circadian rhythm The periodic rhythm of the body, which is synchronised approximately to a 24 hour day/night cycle.

Circulation The movement of fluid through a particular course, especially the passage of blood through the cardio-vascular system.

Classical riding see **Posture**.

Claviceps see **Ergot**.

Cleavers *(Galium aparine)* A straggling annual plant found clinging to hedgerows, common in Britain, Europe and other parts of the world. It has tiny hooks, which attach themselves to clothing, animals, etc. It is used medicinally as a diuretic, and also as a reliable lymphatic alterative.

Clog A piece of wood used to administer medicines. It was coated with the remedy, which was mixed with honey or butter; and was then placed in the horse's mouth like a bit, so that the animal swallowed the medicine gradually.

Clover *(Trifolium spp.)* A nitrogen-producing legume which is recommended for horse pastures. However, exessive amounts of clover should be avoided, since it can be associated with laminitis and with conditions such as photosensitisation. Digestive problems can also arise from the ingestion of mycotoxins of fungi which infect the plant. However, for a variety reasons, including climate, agricultural methods, and possibly the native strains of clover, problems arising from excessive ingestion are rare in Britain. See also **Meadow**.

Clyster A liquid injected into the intestines to treat a medical condition

Coal-tar A thick, black, opaque liquid, formed when coal is distilled.

Cobalt A trace element vital for the synthesis of vitamin B12 in the gut. Available in the horse's natural diet, amounts varying amongst individual foods.

Cocaine *(Erythroxylon coca)* A Peruvian shrub, the leaves of which contain a powerful narcotic and stimulant. Traditionally used as a local anaesthetic, most often for allowing surgical procedures to be carried out without pain. Its use may contravene the rules of competition sport.

Cocksfoot *(Dactylis glomerata)* A species of grass recommended for horse pastures — see **Meadow**.

Cod-liver oil Traditionally used as an alterative and tonic in debilitating illnesses, especially those involving looseness of the bowels. Also used for convalescence and to maintain vigour in older animals. Fish oils are not recommended for routine use unless under the direction of a veterinary surgeon.

Cognitive ethology A humanistic branch of biology which involves the study of character. Research in this area, especially with the higher mammals, indicates that humans are not the only beings to possess a conscience (as well as consciousness), but that some other animals make value judgements concerning their actions. These are not new ideas; a passage from *Horses and Stables* by Sir F. Fitzwygram (1894) reads

It may be said that animals have no sense, no perception of right and wrong; that even their kindness is mere instinct; that certainly, whether they have no perception of right or wrong, they have no means of developing any sense of right and wrong beyond mere instinct. For myself I cannot but believe that there is in every one of the lower* animals a soul, of what nature I know not, but an animal soul appropriate to and suited to the instinct of each.

* At the time of writing the term 'lower animals' generally meant all creatures apart from man. See **Psychology**.

Colchicum autumnale see **Meadow saffron**.

Colic Abdominal pain. May result from several causes, but is often associated with feeding. Colics vary in severity, from a slight upset, which goes of its own accord, to a life-threatening condition, which requires major surgery. The three common types are: spasmodic, which (as the name suggests comes and goes and is generally mild in nature; tympanic, which produces acute continuous pain, high pulse and sweating; obstructive, involving an obstruction of the intestines, usually at the pelvic flexure, which is potentially very serious. See **Holistic feeding stuffs and supplements**, **Twisted gut**.

Collodion A gluey solution of nitrated cotton in alcohol and ether, formerly painted on fresh wounds in order to keep the clean and to exclude the air.

Colostrum The first milk produced after (or sometimes shortly before) parturition. It provides, amongst other things, protective antibodies for the foal.

Coltsfoot *(Tussilago farfara)* A perennial plant that grows on banks, footpaths, damp fields and waste ground in most of Europe, north Asia and north Africa. Traditionally used in herbal remedies to treat coughs.

Columbine *(Aquilegia vulgaris)* A plant found only locally in Britain, although many other hybrids and species are cultivated in gardens. The plant contains alkaloids which are potentially poisonous, but no case of poisoning has been recorded. See **Poisonous plants**.

Coma A state of deep and profound unconsciousness during which the patient cannot be roused and shows no pain reflex response. Coma can be the result of an exessively high temperature, brain injury, etc., or the terminal stage of a fatal illness. Compare **Stupor**.

▶ **Comfrey** *(Symphytum officinale)* A plant commonly found growing in damp conditions, such as riverbanks and marshes, in Europe and Asia. Comfrey has been used for generations to soothe and heal skin wounds, and also to treat fractured bones (thought to be a function of one of its constituents, allantoin), hence its common name 'knitbone'. It can also be used internally to stop bleeding. Some varieties contain pyrrolizidine alkaloids, which have been linked to the formation of tumours. In homoeopathic form it is safe.

Complementary feeding stuff A term defined by the *Feeding Stuffs Regulations 1991* as: 'A mixture of feeding stuffs which has a high content of certain substances and which, by reason of its composition, is sufficient for a daily ration only if it is used in combination with other feeding stuffs'. See **Statutory Statement**, **Complete feeding stuffs.**

Complementary medicine An increasing number of so-called alternative therapies are being accepted by the modern medical establishment: physiotherapy being an example. In these circumstances, the therapy tends to be referred to as 'complementary' rather than 'alternative'. Compare **Alternative medicine**, see **Traditional medicine**, **Holistic therapy**.

Complete feeding stuff A term defined by the *Feeding Stuffs Regulations 1991* as: 'A compound feeding stuff which, by reason of its composition, is sufficient to ensure a daily ration'. See **Statutory Statement**, **Complementary feeding stuff**.

Compound food (compound feeding stuff) Defined by the *Feeding Stuffs Regulations 1991* as: 'A mixture of products of vegetable or animal origin in their natural state, fresh or prepared, or products derived from the industrial processing thereof, or organic or inorganic substances, whether or not containing additives, for oral animal feeding in the form of complete feeding stuffs or complementary feeding stuffs.'

Commercially produced compound foods commonly come as cubes and nuts, which are compressed into uniform shapes, or as coarse mixes. Most (except holistic feeds) contain synthetic materials such as vitamins, by-products, and other inappropriate raw materials. See **Statutory Statement, Holistic feedingstuffs, BAHNM.**

Concentrate (ration) That part of the horse's food which is given to provide extra energy for work. It usually includes ingredients (grains, for example) which are not entirely compatible with the horse's evolved physiology. It should therefore be fed with care in order to avoid digestive and other problems.

Concomitant symptom A symptom which accompanies the major presenting symptom and which is a useful aid to prescribing homoeopathically.

Condy's fluid A traditional proprietary antiseptic, thought to consist of permanganate of potash and water, that was highly regarded and widely used.

Conformation A particular shape or form. Conformation deemed desirable is distinctive in specific breeds, and is partially dependent upon prospective use. Conformation is determined largely by selective breeding

Congenital Describes a condition that is believed to have been present from birth.

Congestion Excessive accumulation of blood in tissues or organ.

Conium maculatum see **Hemlock.**

Constitutional remedy One which takes into account the entire make-up of the patient, rather than the presenting symptoms and concomitants alone. It matches the pattern of an individual body's programmed response to disease. This type of remedy has a significant effect on every organ system, including the mind. See also **Polychrest**.

Consultant A specialist in a particular field, whose opinion is sought by others. A veterinary consultant is, by definition, a qualified veterinary surgeon. However, there is a growing trend for those who are not medically qualified to use the term 'consultant'; for example, nutritionists It should be borne in mind that it is illegal for any person who is not a veterinary surgeon to diagnose or treat sick animals.

Contagious Traditionally, a disease which may only be spread by direct physical contact. Now taken to mean any communicable disease.

Contra-indication A term used in medicine to describe any factor in a patient's condition that makes it unwise to pursue a certain line of treatment. Compare **Indication**.

Contusion A bruise.

Convalescent A term used (especially in herbal medicine) to describe a substance that speeds recovery during convalescence.

Conventional medicine A term used to describe what is presently taught in veterinary schools with regard to the use of modern drug medicine. Compare **Alternative medicine**.

COPD (Chronic obstructive pulmonary disease) see **Small airway disease**.

Copper A trace element available in the horse's natural diet, quantities varying amongst individual foods. Associated with the formation of bone; also with the utilisation of iron in the production of red blood cells. See **Mineral**.

Cordials   The traditional name for medicines given as drinks.

Coriander *(Coriander sativum)*   An aromatic plant of the carrot family, originating in the eastern Mediterranean, that has been introduced to other countries, including the British Isles. Traditionally used as a mild sedative and digestive.

Corn   1) A general term for grain, or cereal crops (in USA, specifically maize).
2) A bruise to the sole of the foot, occurring at the inner heel.

Corn cockle *(Agrostemma githago)*   An annual plant reaching 30—100cm in height. The Corn cockle is not native to Britain, but was formerly a common weed in cereal crops, as it still is in other parts of the world. The plant contains colloidal glycosides and there are reports of it causing poisoning in horses. It is listed as a poisonous plant — see **Poisonous plants**.

Cornea   The transparent circular membrane that forms the front covering of the eyeball.

Corrosive   The term formerly used to describe caustic substances which were used as an antiseptic/disinfectant.

Corrosive sublimate   A chemical preparation (mercuric chloride) formerly used as a corrosive antiseptic and disinfectant, and to promote healing of difficult wounds. Also used to disinfect surgical instruments and the hands of the operator prior to surgery.

Corticosteroid   A steroidal agent produced by the adrenal cortex, or a synthesised analogue of this. Anti-inflammatory and highly suppresive in action.

Couch grass *(Agropyron repens)*   Also known as creeping twitch or dog's grass. A weed of arable and waste land; common in the British Isles. Traditionally believed to be an anthelmintic.

Counter-irritant see **Blistering and rowelling**.

Cowbane *(Cicuta virosa)* An erect perennial plant reaching 30—130cm in height. Prefers damp locations such as shallow water, ditches, and marshes. It is found in localised areas of Britain such as East Anglia, small parts of the Midlands, some parts of Scotland and Ireland. The roots contain a concentrated convulsive poison, and small quantities of it can kill a horse. Listed as a poison — see **Poisonous plants**.

Cradle A device to restrict downward and sideways movement of the horse's head to prevent biting of dressings, clothing, etc. Made from five or six rods, the length of the horse's neck, which are fastened together at intervals with two straps, top and bottom, to form a cradle. This is placed around the neck and secured — see also **Side rod**.

Crani- Prefix denoting the skull.

Crataegus monogyna see **Hawthorn**.

Creeping red fescue *(Festuca rubra)* A species of grass recommended for horse pastures — see **Meadow**.

Creosote A distillation of coal tar, having antiseptic properties. Traditionally used in preparations for inhalation in the treatment of respiratory ailments, and in antiseptic and anti-parasitic ointment. Also used widely for preserving timber, it is potentially dangerous if ingested in large quantities.

Crested dog's tail *(Cynosurus cristatus)* A species of grass recommended for horse pastures — see **Meadow**.

Croton eleuteria see **Cascarilla**.

Croton oil An oil extracted from the seeds of a tropical plant of the spurge family. Formerly used as a purgative.

Cruelty Deliberately causing distress or injury, or failing to take reasonable action to prevent or alleviate distress or injury.

Crystal violet An antiseptic used for infected wounds, burns, fungal skin infections and chronic ulcers. See also **Gentian violet**.

Cubebs The dried berries of a Sumatran climbing shrub, *Piper cubeba*, traditionally used as a digestive stimulant. Otherwise known as Java pepper.

Cubes see **Compound food**.

Culpeper, Nicholas (1616–1654) Physician and astrologer remembered for his herbal: *The English Physician Enlarged, with 369 medicines made of English herbs*, which was widely read and used until the nineteenth century.

Curb An enlargement of the plantar ligament which runs down the back of the hock joint.

Cure The total elimination of disease and restoration of health.

Cyanocobalmin Vitamin B12 – see **Vitamins**.

Cyanosis Blueing of mucous membranes and other tissues.

Cynosurus cristatus see **Crested dog's tail**.

Cyst An abnormal sac or enclosed cavity containing liquid or semi-solid matter. Cysts can occur in many parts of the body.

Dactylis glomorata see **Cocksfoot**.

Daffy's elixir see **Tincture**.

Daisy *(Bellis perennis)* A perennial plant growing to some 15cm, common in grassland and lawns. Used medicinally in the homoeopathic treatment of sprains, bruises and eczema. The daisy is recommended for horse pastures —see **Meadow**.

▶ **Dandelion** *(Taraxacum officinale)* A plant common in meadows, pastures, fields and waste ground throughout Europe. There are numerous sub-species. The common name 'pee in the bed' is consistent with its powerful diuretic properties. It is used in herbal medicine to clear the blood of impurities, and as a mild laxative and bitter tonic. Dandelion is recommended for horse pastures.

Dandruff A condition whereby the skin becomes scaly, producing fragments which cling to the coat. There are many causes, including poor diet and some diseases.

Darnel *(Lolium temulentum)* An erect annual grass which reaches a height of about 1m. Darnel is the only British grass which is harmful but, although it used to be a common weed in cereal crops, it is now rare. There are many accounts from ancient times of people and animals being poisoned by eating food made from flour contaminated with darnel seeds. Although its poisonous principle is not clear, it is thought to be associated with alkaloids. It is listed as a poison - see **Poisonous plants**.

Datura stramonium see **Thorn apple**

Deadly nightshade see **Belladona**.

Decimal Scale of dilution of a homoeopathic remedy, each stage being one in ten.

Decoction A herbal remedy for oral administration made by boiling plants in water. Generally used when trying to extract substances from the harder, woody parts of plants, such as the roots. The material is usually crushed or ground and boiled vigorously before being allowed to cool for the horse to drink.

Defecation The expulsion of faeces through the anus.

Dehydration Loss or deficiency of water in the body. This may arise from exessive sweating, vomiting or diarrhoea and/or from inadequate water intake.

Delphinium see **Larkspur**.

Demulcent An agent which soothes and protects irritated tissues, especially the mucous membranes.

Dentine The hard tissue which makes up the bulk of the tooth.

Depurative A term used (especially in herbal medicine) to describe a substance that cleanses and purifies the system, especially the blood.

Dermatitis Inflammation of the skin.

Dermatophyte Skin fungus, for example ringworm.

Destructive remedy A homoeopathic term for a remedy in which the 'picture' is of tissue destruction.

Detergent A cleansing agent that removes impurities from a surface by reacting with grease and suspended particles, including micro-organisms. Detergent powders formerly used to cleanse foul ulcers consisted of such substances as blue vitriol (hydrated copper sulphate), bole armenion (made from a red clay), and alum. Detergent ointments were also prepared from similar ingredients and employed for the same purpose.

Devil's claw *(Harpagophytum procumbens)* The tuber of a prostrate perennial plant with spiked and barbed fruits, which grows in Namibia, Botswana and South Africa. It is used in herbal medicine as an anti-inflammatory and analgesic. The physiological action of Devil's claw has been compared to the powerful modern synthetic drugs, cortisone and phenyl-butazone. It should not be used in some circumstances, such as during pregnancy. Its use may contravene the rules of competition sport.

Dextrose see **Glucose**.

Diachylon Also known as litharge or lead plaster. A plaster made from plant juices and other ingredients, formerly used to stiffen leather in order to protect a sensitive part of the anatomy from pressure. It was applied as a liquid and formed a plaster when dry.

Diagnosis The art of distinguishing one disease from another, or of determining the nature of the disease.

Diapente A powder traditionally used in stomachic and tonic remedies, containing bay, gentian root, birthwort and hart's horn.

Diaphoretics A term used (especially in herbal medicine) to describe substances which promote perspiration in the form of vapour. They are called sudorifics if sweat appears in noticeable drops.

Diaphragm The thin, dome-shaped muscle that separates the thoracic and abdominal cavities.

Diarrhoea Frequent bowel evacuation, or the passage of abnormally soft or liquid faeces. Causes include intestinal infections, other forms of intestinal inflammation, and anxiety.

Diathesis Constitution or condition of the body which

predisposes it to a certain type of disease reaction.

Digestion The process by which food is converted into a form that can be absorbed and assimilated by the body. Compare **Indigestion**; see **Colic**.

Digestive A term used (especially in herbal medicine) to describe a substance that aids digestion.

Digitalis purpurea/lanata see **Foxglove**.

Dioscorides A citizen of the Roman Empire who wrote extensive treatises which included information on medicinal plants. His *Materia Medica* (AD 77) included advice on the cultivation and use of around 600 species, and it was widely used by physicians in sebsequent centuries.

Disease Dynamic disturbance of the harmony existing between the 'vital force' in a body and the material body itself. Literally dis-ease.

Disinfectant An agent which removes or destroys organisms, such as bacteria, which are capable of infecting the body. Disinfectants are generally not applied to the body or ingested, since they may be toxic or corrosive.

Distal Situated away from the centre of the body. Thus the foot is distal to the cannon bone. Compare **Proximal**.

Diuresis Increased excretion of urine.

Diuretic A substance that increases the production of urine. A valuable herbal diuretic is the dandelion *(Taraxacum officinale)*, which is reputed to be as powerful as modern synthetic diuretics, and is potentially safer, owing to its high potassium content.

DJD (Degenerative joint disease) A generic term for a

variety of conditions involving arthritis in the joints. DJD develops for a number of reasons and is closely related to over-straining the joints during hard work. Holistic nutrition and medicine are often successful in management of the problem.

DNA (Deoxyribonucleic acid) The genetic material of living organisms which controls heredity. Located in the cell nucleus, the DNA molecule can make exact copies of itself, thereby passing on genetic information when the cell divides.

Docking Removal of part of the horse's tail, which was practised in England as early as medieval times. It was widely used for harness horses at the beginning of the eighteenth century. Although, originally, docking possibly had some practical value, it was later carried out largely for reasons of fashion. Docking was made illegal in England in 1948.

Doctor In human medicine, when someone describes themselves as 'a doctor' there is little doubt about the meaning of the word: it implies 'physician'. Likewise, in the animal field the term 'veterinary surgeon' denotes someone who is qualified to practise animal medicine. It is when the letters 'Dr' are used as a prefix to someone's name that confusion can arise.What this signifies is that the person has obtained a doctorate degree, which could be in any discipline. Such people, either in the human or animal fields, may or may not be qualified to practise medicine. Veterinary surgeons, who are not normally styled 'Dr' in the UK, usually indicate their qualification to practise medicine by the use of the letters MRCVS or FRCVS after their name (Member or Fellow of the Royal College of Veterinary Surgeons).

Doctor Green Traditionally a reference to good meadows. Horses recovering from illness or injury were often put out to recuperate in fields where they could forage for the herbage they required. See **Meadow**.

Dover's powder A traditional diaphoretic consisting of

opium, ipecacuanha, and potash sulphate.

Dragon's blood A red, resinous exudation from the dragon tree *(Dracaena draco)*, which is found in the Canary Islands. Formerly used as an astringent and styptic.

Drenching A liquid medicine given by mouth, administered whilst the horse's head is held up, so that he has little option but to swallow it.

Drown, Ruth An American chiropractor, who, whilst practising in Hollywood in the 1930s, developed a new and more sophisticated form of radionics treatment. This involved both diagnosis and treatment of disease from a distance. See **Radionics**.

Drug Any substance which can affect the structure or function of the body. The term is normally used to describe modern pharmaceutical medicines, whereas the term 'remedy' is normally used to describe herbal or 'natural' medicines.

Dry matter basis Calculations for the amount of food to give are often made on a 'dry matter basis'. This means that the weight of the moisture in the food should be deducted from the equation.

Dryopteris filix-mas see **Male fern**.

Dynamics A study of the activity of the body and the forces involved.

Dysentery Inflammation of the intestines involving the passing of blood, mucus or bowel lining with the dung.

Dyspnoea Difficulty in breathing.

Easton's syrup A traditional medicine prepared from nux vomica *(Strychnos nux vomica)*.

Ecbolic An agent that induces contraction of the uterus, leading to parturition.

Echinacea *(Echinacea angustifolia)* A plant originating from western USA, which is cultivated as an ornamental species in Europe. It grows in dry, open woodland and on prairies. Echinacea is valued in herbal medicine for its immuno-stimulant and antibiotic properties. It is also valued in homoeopathy for supporting recovery from viral infections, and for treating skin problems.

-ectomy Suffix denoting surgical removal of an organ or part.

Ectoparasite A parasite that lives on the outer surface of its host. See **Parasite**; compare **Endoparasite.**

Eczema Superficial inflammation of the skin. Eczema causes itching, with a red rash, and is often accompanied by weeping areas, which become encrusted.

Eggs Hens' eggs were formerly used as a general tonic in food and also for mixing oils and balsams with water. Eggs can cause dietary imbalance in horses, and their use is not recommended except under veterinary supervision.

Egyptiacum A traditional remedy for dressing wounds, containing verdigris, blue vitriol and honey. Various other ingredients such as alum and vinegar were also used.

Elbers Papyrus One of the best records of ancient medical practices, the Elbers Papyrus came to light in 1862, when the archaeologist Georg Elbers purchased it from a wealthy Egyptian. The manuscript, written around 1500BC, contains a wealth of information on ancient Egyptian pharmacy, including references to over 800 remedies involving the use of medicinal plant extracts, animal organs and minerals. Many of the remedies, such as the use of castor oil to treat constipation, were obviously efficacious and have stood the test of time.

I ▶   **Elder** *(Sambucus nigra)*   A deciduous shrub common on waste ground and in woods and hedgerows; found in most of Europe, western Siberia, the Caucasus and Turkey. The leaves were formerly boiled in lard to produce an emollient, which was used to treat inflamed and irritated areas.

Elecampane *(Inula helenium)*   A composite plant allied to the aster, formerly cultivated widely for its medicinal properties and traditionally used as a respiratory stimulant.

Electrolytes   Usually a reference to those salts, principally sodium and chlorine, with lesser amounts of potassium, calcium and magnesium, that the horse loses during perspiration.

Electro-therapy   The treatment of disease and injury by the use of electricity. This is done either by direct application to the skin surface, or by placing the affected area in an electro-magnetic or electrical field.

Galvanism was probably the first type of electro-therapy used. The process is named after Luigi Galvani who, in 1789, performed a famous experiment involving a freshly dissected frog's leg, which twitched when stimulated with electricity. Galvanism is now used to improve the flow of blood at the site of an injury.

Farradism was developed by Michael Faraday in the early part of the nineteenth century. He used an apparatus employing electro-magnetic fields to produce pulsating electrical currents with varying pulse shapes, frequencies and durations. His developments make it possible to estimate the degree of nerve and muscle damage which result from injury.

When used properly as part of a holistic approach to medicine, electro-therapy can be very effective. It is not a system of medicine in its own right.

Electuary Traditionally, a mixture of medicines made into a paste with treacle, honey or the like. A convenient method of applying remedies to the throat or pharynx by smearing th preparation onto the back of the tongue or teeth with a flat stick. A traditional electuary for a sore throat is extract of belladonna, potassium chlorate and aniseed, mixed with treacle. Other types of electuary were used for the internal treatment of conditions such as intestinal problems. For example, electuary of senna, containing senna, coriander, figs, licorice, prunes, tamarind and sugar was a popular laxative.

Elemi gum A fragrant, resinous substance extracted from various tropical trees such as *Canarium*. Formerly used for digestive ailments.

Embrocation A lotion (sometimes called linament), usually oily, that is rubbed on to the body for the treatment of painful muscular conditions, strains and sprains. Linaments are usually of a poisonous nature, for example the traditional 'ABC linament' consists of aconite, belladonna, and chloroform.

Emetic A substance that causes vomiting (not appropriate for horses).

Emmenagogue The term used for an agent that stimulates menstruation.

Emollient An agent that gives suppleness and softens the skin, examples being lanolin and liquid paraffin.

Emphysema Pathological accumulation of air or gas in the tissues, particularly when air leaks into the tissues from lung air spaces.

Endemic Occurring frequently in a particular region or population. The term is applied to diseases constantly or generally present in a particular place.

Endoparasite   A parasite that lives inside its host, for example in the intestines or other tissues of the body. See **Parasite**, compare **Ectoparasite**.

Endorphine   One of a group of substances which occur naturally in the body, having pain-relieving properties similar in action to the opiates. The body can be prompted to produce endorphines by the stimulation of acupuncture points; it is thought that the use of the twitch has the same effect.

Endoscope   An instrument used to obtain a view of the inside of the body. Most endoscopes consist of a tube with a light on the end, and an optical system for transmitting an image to the eye of the examiner.

Enema   A quantity of fluid injected into the rectum through a tube passed into the anus.

Enteric   Relating to or affecting the intestine.

Enteritis   Inflammation of the intestine, usually causing diarrhoea.

Enzootic   A disease (usually transmissible) which exists among an animal population and which usually reaches a balance with the population.

Enzyme   A protein that acts as a catalyst, increasing the rate of a biological action. For example, digestive enzymes break down food into substances small enough to be absorbed across the gut wall. Enymes are essential for the normal functioning and development of the body.

I ▶   **Eohippus**   Eohippus or 'dawn horse' is widely regarded as the first 'true' horse; the forerunner of the modern counterpart. He existed about 55 million years ago, was about the size of a fox, and had four toes on each forefoot and three on each hind foot. Eohippus inhabited semi-forested areas and lived on a varied diet, which included berries and soft fruits.

Epidemiology The study of epidemic disease with a view to finding a means of control and future prevention.

Epidermis The outer layer of skin, which is continually being sloughed off and replaced by new tissues from beneath.

Epistaxis Bleeding from the nose.

Epizootic A disease (usually transmissible) which is not in balance with an animal population and is spreading.

Epsom salts Epsomite is a mineral, hydrated magnesium sulphate. Epsom salts is of similar composition, and was originally obtained from the springs at Epsom in Surrey, England. Traditionally used as a laxative and purgative (action in the latter use uncertain), and also for liver and respiratory problems.

Equilibrium A state of balance in which all forces exactly counteract each other.

Equine herpes virus A virus which causes symptoms similar to equine influenza: runny nose and high temperature, with the glands of the head and neck sometimes becoming slightly enlarged. Certain strains of the virus can cause abortion.

Equine influenza An acute respiratory disease caused by a virus which gains entry into the respiratory tract through the nose, and settles in the linings of the trachea and bronchioles. Symptoms of the disease include elevated temperature, coughing, and a nasal discharge. One of the problems with this type of infection is not so much the virus itself, but the damage it does in laying the way open for secondary infections.

Vaccination is often used in an attempt to prevent the disease, but can bring on its own problems in sensitive individuals. It should be noted that vaccination is a requirement for many of the sporting disciplines. Annual boosting is not proven necessary by science.

Homoeopathic and herbal preventative methods can be effective and safe if carried out under properly qualified and experienced veterinary supervision. Proper nutrition is also very important to the immune system.

Equisetum arvense see **Horsetail**.

Ergot 1) *(Claviceps)* A type of fungus that infects with varying severity many species of cereal crops. The fungus can be seen protruding from infected seed heads as hard masses called 'ergots'. These are poisonous and, although seen infrequently today, they were formerly seen in many crops of rye. Ergot of rye was used in traditional medicine to constrict the small blood vessels, being given to mares after parturition, and used to treat inflammation of the coverings of the brain and spinal column. The material can be used in extreme dilutions in homoeopathy.

I 2) A horny growth at the back of the fetlock joint. A remnant of a pad behind the toe of an ancestor of the horse.

Errhines Substances that cause sneezing. Formerly, various powders of substances such as hellebore and snuff were blown up the nostrils for this purpose.

Erythroxylon coca see **Cocaine**.

Essential amino acids see **Amino acid**.

Essential oils Volatile substances obtained from plants, usually having a characteristic, and often aromatic, smell.

They are easily taken up by water vapour or steam. The umbellifer and legume families contain many plants with essential oils. See also **Aromatherapy**.

Ether A volatile liquid having a marked effect on the heart, formerly used as an anaesthetic by inhalation; also given by subcutaneous injection. Traditionally used in colic draughts.

Eucalyptus *(Eucalyptus globus)* A large, characteristically Australian forest tree of the myrtle family, yielding timber, oils and gum. Traditional medicinal use of the oil is as a remedy to stimulate the respiratory system, administered as a vapour to be inhaled. It is also used as an antiseptic.

Eugenics In homoeopathy, the treatment of the unborn in the womb as an attempt to eliminate disease acquired as a result of maternal ill-health or miasmic influence.

Euphorbium A gum resin obtained from the spurge genus of plants. Formerly used for blistering and to reduce callouses.

Euthanasia A means of producing death free from anti-mortem fear or suffering. Although, for most owners, the decision to have a sick horse destroyed is an agonising one, it is a responsibility that should not be shirked. It is in the best interests of the horse for euthanasia to be carried out in surroundings with which he is entirely familiar, and it must be carried out by a competent and qualified person. Anaesthetics are often used nowadays, under veterinary care.

Excretion Removal from the body of the waste products of metabolism. Compare **Secretion**.

Exercise Correct exercise entails a gradual and patient increase of demands upon the muscles, tendons, ligaments, respiratory system and heart. Through this process, the body is brought to a condition which will properly support hard work. Without such a progression, the organs and tissues would be totally incapable of withstanding the pressures of hard work.

Exhalation The act of expelling air from the lungs. Compare **Inhalation**.

Exostoses Bony protuberances.

Expectorant A substance that promotes expulsion of mucus from the respiratory tract. Expectorants act by increasing the bronchial secretion, or by making it less viscous and easier to cough up.

Extrusion A method of cooking and preparing food, most commonly grains, for horses and other animals. The food is impregnated with steam and forced through metal dies, thus producing the familiar nugget-shaped lumps. The high temperature reached during this process destroys the majority of vitamins and other micro-nutrients, and feeds prepared in this way are commonly fortified with synthetic products. See **Holistic feeding stuffs and supplements**.

Faculty of Homoeopathy An organisation established by Act of Parliament to promote and teach medical homo-eopathy. It accredits courses for physicians and veterinary surgeons and sets an examination for veterinarians which, when passed, confers the qualification Vet. M.F. Hom.The Fellows of the Faculty are entitled to the designation Vet. F.F. Hom.

Faeces Waste material that is expelled from the digestive system through the anus.

Fahrenheit temperature Temperature expressed on a scale by which the melting point of ice is assigned a value of 32 degrees and the boiling point of water a value of 212 degrees. Named after the inventor, G. D. Fahrenheit (1686–1736), a German physicist. Compare **Centigrade**.

Faradism see **Electro-therapy**.

Farcy see **Glanders**.

Farrier The term farrier is used today for a shoeing smith — see **Shoes**. However, in the days before veterinary surgery existed as a profession, the farrier was the principal horse doctor, charged with the responsibility of administering medicines to sick horses. The variety of treatments given for various ailments was endless, with recipes for potions being handed down from father to son. Initially, these contained relatively simple ingredients, similar to those used in the human medicine of the time. However, as materials from other countries became more available, remedies became more exotic. The principles for their use were also influenced by foreign cultures, and many strange and unfathomable substances were available to the 'horse doctor'. While some of these were useful, containin ingredients which are the basis of modern veterinary medicines, a great number were useless or dangerous, being formulated by 'quacks'.

Fasciculation Localised twitching of individual bunches of muscle fibres.

Fat The means by which the body stores surplus energy; fat also serves as an insulating material beneath the skin and around certain internal organs.Normal body fat consists of substances known as glycerides.

Feather The long hair on the fetlocks of certain breeds such as Shires and Clydesdales.

Febrifuge see **Anti-pyretic**.

Feeding Stuffs Regulations *The Feeding Stuffs Regulations 1991*, with subsequent amendments, is a Statutory Instrument of the Government. It sets out the regulations which must be followed by manufacturers of all animal feeding stuffs. The regulations are under constant review by the Ministry of Agriculture, Fisheries and Food, and there are some eighty pages of regulations arranged in various schedules.

Certain information about a feed product must be declared in a prescribed way on the product packaging. This includes the nature of the raw materials used. Unfortunately, under the Regulations, this information may legally be expressed in a way which is not readily understood by the average consumer. Consequently, the use of by-products, artificial ingredients and the like may go unnoticed. This means that consumers wishing to avoid such ingredients are unable to make an informed choice. See **Holistic feeding stuffs and supplements**, **Statutory Statement**.

Feed supplements see **Nutritional supplements**.

Fenugreek *(Trigonella foenum-graecum)* A plant which grows in countries around the eastern Mediterranean and is cultivated throughout the Middle East. Fenugreek has been used for generations as a fodder crop. Its use in nutrition and medicine dates back to the time of the ancient Egyptians and Hippocrates. It may be given to healthy horses on a regular basis as a conditioner, being good for weight gain, coat and hooves. Because it is a uterine stimulant it should not be given to pregnant mares, but it may be given to nursing mares to promote milk flow.

Fern see **Male fern**.

Fertiliser A substance that encourages plant growth. One of the major causes of the depletion of herbal species in modern grassland is the use of artificial fertilisers. These encourage the faster- growing grasses at the expense of the slower-growing herbage, which is smothered. They also cause chemical imbalances, including depletion of trace minerals, in the soil. Natural manure, consisting of the droppings of farm animals such as cows, releases its goodness slowly. This allows a more natural growth of flora, thereby preserving species diversity. Calcified seaweed is also a useful fertiliser. See also **Meadow**. N.B. The BAHNM will provide information on holistic pasture management.

Ferula asafoetida see **Asafoetida**.

Festuca rubra see **Creeping red fescue**.

Fever A rise in body temperature above normal; one of the commonest symptoms of infectious disease. Holistic medicine sees the fever not simply as something to be reduced, but as an opportunity to strengthen the body's emergency defences. The aim is to shorten the fever by improving its efficiency, at the same time providing remedies which will reduce excessive symptoms associated with the struggle.

Fever in the feet see **Laminitis**.

Fibrin A proteinatious substance upon which depends the formation of blood clots – thus vital in the natural arrest of bleeding. The clotting process is very complex; jelly-like clots are formed by minute threads of fibrin, in which are enmeshed red blood corpuscles, white blood cells and platelets.

Field From the old English word 'feld', which meant felled area. Grazing for animals was originally created by clearing areas of ancient woodland. Being unploughed they could support many different varieties of grasses and herbage which sprung from the undisturbed earth below. See also **Meadow**.

Figs The fruit of a tree of the Mulberry family *(Ficus),* traditionally used as a laxative.

Fillipendula ulmaria see **Meadowsweet**.

Filled legs A condition of the legs where there is more or less swelling. This is caused by fluid which accumulates under the skin for a variety of reasons. The swelling has a soft, doughy consistency, and is usually quick to disperse when the horse is exercised. There is often no pain or heat associated with the condition and it does not interfere with the horse's action, except perhaps for a slight initial stiffeness. Some horses are more prone to filled legs than others; nutrition and level of fitness are predisposing factors.

Firing Hot-iron firing was the application of smouldering metal firing irons to the site of an injury to the limbs (as opposed to their use in cauterising tissue). The theory was that the treatment produced 'beneficial swelling and counter-irritation' (see **Blistering and rowelling**) to the affected part. The other benefit was thought to be that the scar tissue so formed would be stronger than the original, and would act like a permanent bandage This was of particular relevance to tendon injuries. The practice is no longer recommended by the Royal College of Veterinary Surgeons.

Acid firing was based on the same principles as hot-iron firing, and used for similar problems. This method, practised for centuries by the Arabs, involved the application of strong sulphuric acid to the skin. It enjoyed a brief revival in the 1950s. Acid firing was generally thought preferable to hot-iron firing, as most practitioners felt it caused little pain and could therefore be used without anaesthetic. Most leg injuries respond well to laser therapy, proper exercise and homoeopathic and herbal medication.

First aid The first action taken to help a patient after injury. In the case of all but minor injuries, the veterinary surgeon should be contacted. In an emergency it may be necessary to follow telephoned instructions prior to the vet's arrival.

A first aid/medicines kit should always be available; its contents should be checked regularly and replenished as necessary. The following list outlines a basic kit which is compatible with holistic principles:

<u>General</u>: emergency number for veterinary surgeon; pencil

and paper; thermometer; scissors; small bowl; tweezers; large syringe (for flushing out wounds with saline solution); 10% saline solution; cotton wool; gamgee; comfrey poultice; bandages; antiseptic wound powder.

Homoeopathic remedies (6c). If liquid, apply to inside of lower lip or give in water; if pillules, give in piece of apple or carrot:

Arnica montana — helps minimise the immediate effects of physical injury.

Aconitum napellus — for fevers.

Nux vomica — for digestive problems.

Colocynthis — for severe abdominal pain.

Arsenicam — for intestinal discomfort and diarrhoea.

Rhus toxicodendron — for the relief of rheumatic pain.

Ruta graveolens — for sprain or dislocation.

Hepar sulphuris — for supperating wounds.

Ledum — for puncture wounds.

Hypericum — reduces pain in lacerated injuries

Creams and lotions:

Hypericum / Calendula lotion for cuts, bruises and wounds.

Arnica cream/lotion

Fish meal   Dried, powdered fish derivatives, sometimes used in foal creep feeds and mares milk replacer as a source of protein. Being incompatible with the evolved physiology of horses, its use is contrary to the principles of holistic nutrition. See **Holistic feeding stuffs and supplements**.

Fish oils   see **Cod-liver oil**.

Fistulous withers   An infection which develops in connection with the withers, often as a result of mechanical injury, such as may be caused by pressure from the harness or a badly fitting saddle.

Fitness   Although fitness is a relative term, a fit horse is thought of as one being sound in wind and limb and capable of vigorous exercise without undue fatigue or signs of physical incapacity. The condition of the respiratory organs, together with the general condition of the body — especially the limbs — are factors central to the fitness of the horse. The provision of optimum nutrition together with a proper exercise routine are essential to maintaining fitness — see **Holistic feeding stuffs and supplements**.

Flaccid Weak, lax or soft.

Flatulence The production of gas in the bowel or stomach; often associated with diet.

Flavonoids and bio-flavonoids Chemical constituents of plants. Most herbs containing flavonoids are diuretic; some are antispasmodic, and others are anti-inflammatory. Bio-flavonoids are known to strengthen the capilliaries, and are useful in the treatment of conditions which arise as a result of vulnerable tissue.

Flavourings Flavourings are sometimes added to compounded horse feed in order to make it more palatable. The flavourings are usually artificial and, as such, incompatible with the evolved physiology of the horse and therefore contrary to the principles of holistic nutrition. Their use is entirely unnecessary if appropriate raw materials are used to formulate the ration. See **BAHNM**, **Holistic feeding stuffs and supplements**.

Flax refers to the fibrous parts of some plants, or to the plants themselves, for example linseed and Indian hemp.

Flehmen position An extension of the horse's head and neck, together with a curling of the upper lip. Most commonly associated with entire males who are stimulated by the scent of a female, but also seen in mares and geldings. It is thought that the increased exposure of the mucous membrane of the mouth traps additional scent-carrying particles. The Flehmen response may also be stimulated by non-sexual smells such as that of garlic.

Fleming, Alexander see **Penicillin**.

Flowers of sulphur A preparation of sulphur, traditionally used in the treatment of many ailments, notably for mange. Also used as a mild aperient, alterative and diaphoretic. Greatly valued by horsemen as a 'conditioner' and for producing a glossy coat.

Folic acid A vitamin of the B complex – see **Vitamins**.

Fomentation Strictly, the application of heat and moisture to the skin with a flannel, or by similar means. Bathing any part with warm water is known as 'fomenting'.

Food allergies see **Allergy**.

Forge water A favourite remedy used in traditional farriery. Containing iron, it was given as a tonic.

Forging The term used to describe the toe of a hind foot striking the sole of a forefoot when the horse is in motion. Indicative of faulty action, lack of balance or fatigue.

Formaldehyde A derivative of formic acid, used as a vapour in the fumigation of buildings etc.

Formalin A powerful antiseptic, prepared by the oxidation of methyl alchohol. It is used for preserving pathological specimens and, occasionally, as a disinfectant. Also used in the production of formaldehyde gas for fumigation.

Fortification (of food) An attempt to restore the nutritional value of food when constituents have been damaged or destroyed by processing. The process of fortification usually involves the addition of synthetic products — see **By-products**, **Vitamins**.

Founder see **Laminitis**.

Fowler's solution A traditional proprietary solution of arsenic, otherwise known as ***Liquor arsenicalis***, administered in the horse's food.

I ► **Foxglove** *(Digitalis purpurea / lanata)* An erect biennial plant reaching 1.5m in height, found growing throughout Europe. The leaves of the purple foxglove are the source of digitalis. When dried and finely ground this can be made into an infusion which affects the heart by increasing the force of the heartbeat whilst lessening the frequency of beats. It can also be used to excite the kidneys to produce more urine than usual. Poisonous doses send the heart into spasm, and death is caused by cardiac paralysis. Foxglove is listed as a poison (*see **Poisonous plants***), but it is a valuable homoeopathic remedy in correct dosage.

Fracture Complete or incomplete breakage of a bone. The natural ability of the body to repair fractures can be greatly stimulated through correct nutrition and the use of herbal and homoeopathic medicines — see **Comfrey**.

Frangula alnus see **Alder buckthorn**.

Friar's balsam see **Balsams**.

Fumigation The use of gasses such as formaldehyde or chlorine to disinfect clothing, buildings etc. Care must be taken to ensure minimal toxicity to horses and personnel.

Fungus One of the simplest forms of plant, lacking the green pigment, chlorophyll. Fungi include such organisms as mushrooms, yeasts, and moulds. Moulds are the source of many modern antibiotics, including as penicillin, which is obtained from the mould *Penicillium chrysogenum*.

Fungal diseases, broadly speaking, include both the invasion of tissue by fungi (see **Ringworm**), and the effects on the organs of fungal poisons such as mycotoxins (see **Ergot**).

Fungi such as aspergillus thrive in dusty hay and straw

and often cause localised infections of the upper respiratory tract. Fungal spores can also be the cause of allergic tissue reactions in chronic respiratory diseases.

Gadfly (*Tabanidae*) A large and important family of flies; the females are blood suckers and may carry disease. The bite is painful and causes irritation and 'gadding' (rushing here and there in an uncontrolled manner). The term gadfly is sometimes applied to the bot fly.

Gag An instrument placed between the teeth in order to keep the mouth open — see **Balling iron**.

Galactagogue Describes an agent that increases milk flow.

Galangal see **Galingale**.

Galbanum A gum-resin obtained from an Eastern plant of the species *Ferula*. Formerly used as an expectorant.

Galen A Greek (c.129-199 AD) who left an indelible mark on the history of medicine. He studied anatomy and medicine for 12 years, before working as surgeon in the gladiatorial school in Pergamum. He then moved to Rome and practised as a physician and druggist to the aristocracy. He provided the first accurate information on the structure of the nervous system, the secretory function of the kidneys, and the circulation of the blood.

Galingale The aromatic root stock of certain East Indian plants of the ginger family, formerly used much like ginger.

Gall A painful sore or swelling caused by chafing of, for example, the girth or saddle.

Galton's law The theory of ancestral contribution, originally expounded by Sir Frances Galton (1822-1911), which states that the two parents contribute one half each to the progeny;

the four grandparents one quarter each, etc.

Galvanism see **Electro-therapy**.

Gamboge A yellow gum-resin obtained from trees of the genus *Garcina,* indigenous to south-east Asia. Formerly used as an anthelmintic.

Gamgee Cotton wool covered with gauze, usually employed under bandages.

Gammy legs An old term for legs affected by swelling or filling, particularly around tendons. Also called 'gummy legs'

Gangrene Death and decay of part of the body resulting from cessation of the blood supply. See also **Gas gangrene**.

Garden nightshade see **Black nightshade**.

Gargles Liquid remedies, formerly used to treat the mucous membranes of the throat. The horse's head was raised and a small quantity was poured into the back of the mouth. Because of the animal's reluctance to swallow, the liquid remained in contact with the target area until the head was lowered.

Garlic *(Allium sativum)* A herb, originally from Asia, now common in Europe and elsewhere, where it is mainly cultivated (cultivated in Egypt for the past 5000 years). Garlic may be fed regularly to healthy horses as a pure herb. It has a wide spectrum of beneficial effects on the body. It is a good digestive aid, and a good 'warming' remedy for use during winter. It is used medicinally in combination with other herbs as an effective antibiotic, anti-parasitic, expectorant and anti-histamine.

Several other members of the garlic family *(Allium)* may be found growing wild in much of Europe.

Gas gangrene An acute bacterial disease caused by infection from any of the 'gas gangrene' group of bacteria *(Clostridia)*, which cause putrefactive decay of connective tissue. Infection usually occurs via a small wound. The disease takes its name from the generation of gas in the infected tissue.

Gastric Relating to or affecting the stomach.

Gastrophilus see **Bots**.

Generals Symptoms applying to the whole body.

Generic name In pharmacy, the name of a chemical substance, rather than its brand name. Compare **Proprietary name**.

Gentian *(Gentiana lutea)* A herb which is found in the Alps and other mountains of central and south-eastern Europe. Gentian is a pronounced bitter digestive stimulant, containing one of the most bitter substances known — the glycoside, amarogentin. It increases the appetite by stimulating the flow of the digestive juices and bile. In combination with various other substances, gentian has traditionally been used as a general tonic for horses. It is also used to treat cases of gastro-intestinal inflammation. Prolonged use is not advisable.

Gentian violet A mixture of three dyes; methyl rosaniline, methyl violet, and crystal violet. Used as an antiseptic against fungal and bacterial skin infection, as an anthelmintic and also as a stain for microscopic work.

Genus A term used to describe a classification of animals and plants. A genus consists of several closely related and similar species; for example, the genus *Equus* includes the horse *(Equus cabalus)* and also the zebra *(Equus zebra)*.

Germ Any micro-organism, but especially one that causes disease. See **Pasteur, Louis**.

Gerrard, John (1546-1612) Author of *The Herball, or Generall Historie of Plantes* (1598), which describes various flora and their uses in near-poetic language. For example of tobacco he wrote: ' The drie leaves are used to be taken in a pipe set on fire and suckt into the stomacke, and thrust forth again at the nostrils against the paines of the head, rheumes, aches in any part of the bodie.'

Gestation The period during which a fertilised egg cell develops into a foal ready to be born; about eleven months.

Ginger *(Zingibar officinale)* A plant which is native to Asia and cultivated extensively in the West Indies, Africa and India. The rhizome (root) is the part of the plant normally used for both culinary and medicinal purposes. Ginger is a strong vasodilator and circulatory stimulant. It is also a visceral anti-spasmodic, digestive, carminative and warming agent. Traditionally used in horses to aid expulsion of gas from the gut and as a carminative and also (when mixed with aloes and other purgatives) to prevent griping.

Gingering An old practice of forcing ginger or some other irritant up the horse's rectum to encourage a high tail carriage.

Gland An organ, or group of cells, that is specialised for synthesising and secreting specific fluids. These can be either for use in the body, or for excretion. The term is also used to describe lymph nodes.

Glanders A contagious disease caused by the glanders bacillus *Pseudomonas mallei*, formerly known as *Pfeifferalla mallei*. It can affect animals other than horses, including man, and has been recognised as a serious disease since the time of Hippocrates (c.460–377 BC). Glanders was also known as farcy.

Glaubers salt The popular name for sodium sulphate. Traditionally used as an aperient and sometimes mixed with

Epsom salts or senna for a more drastic action — see **Senna**.

Glucose A simple sugar that is used by the body as an energy source. A constituent of sucrose and starch, both of which provide glucose after digestion.

Glycerine A clear, viscous liquid consisting of the by-products of fats and oils, used in the manufacture of soap. Also used as an emollient in many skin preparations and, traditionally, in the preparation of horse balls.

Glycosides Compounds of glucose and other substances, found in plants. The cardiac glycosides, such as digoxin and digitoxin, derived from the foxglove *(Digitalis purpurea/lanata)*, are traditionally used in the treatment of heart failure. Some glycosides form foam when mixed with water and are highly toxic — see **Saponins**.

Glycyrrhiza glabra see **Licorice**.

Goose grease/oil A fat traditionally used as an ointment or 'unguent' in the treatment of stiff joints, swellings and bruises. Animal fat, such as lard, was also used for the same purpose. Goose grease and oil were superseded during the early part of the twentieth century by lanolin and Vaseline, substances which do not turn rancid.

Grain 1) A single small, hard seed, or corn in general (in England) especially wheat.
2) The smallest British weight in avoirdupois. A unit of mass equal to 1/7000 of a pound (the average weight of a seed of corn).

Gram A unit of mass equal to one thousanth of a kilogram.

Granulation Rounded outgrowths, made up of small blood vessels and connective tissue, which spring up over the surface of healing wounds when the edges do not fit closely.

Grassland see **Meadow**.

Grass sickness A disease which originally acquired its name because of the way in which epidemics were associated with horses having access to grass in the late spring after being housed and fed on hard feed during the winter. The disease is common throughout Britain; it is not just concentrated in Scotland and the north of England, as was commonly believed until fairly recently. The cause of the disease remains a mystery, although it is thought by some to be associated with mycotoxins in grazing. Symptoms, which result from damage to parts of the autonomic nervous system, are: loss of appetite, inability to swallow, colic, bowel stasis, sweating and trembling,

Grease *(Seborrhoea)* A fungal infection *(Dermatophilus congolensis)* of the skin which involves the posterior aspect of the fetlocks and pasterns, particularly of the hind limbs. The skin becomes hot and moist and there is an increased production of sebum, which gives off an unpleasant odour. The condition used to be common in heavy cart horses with abundant feather, for example Shires and Clydesdales. It is generally associated with dirty stables and bad management, although it has been seen in horses kept in good order.

Greenstick The term given to the breaking of a bone where marked separation does not occur. Greenstick fractures occur chiefly in young animals, and the pain caused is quite severe.

Gripe Abdominal pain (associated with colic).

Grooming The purpose of grooming a horse is to keep the coat and skin clean and healthy by removing the waste products of metabolism and discouraging invasion by ectoparasites. Grooming also stimulates the circulation, improves the appearance of the coat and skin, and makes the horse feel refreshed. Although they may enjoy being groomed, horses who are turned out and not worked do not normally require the same amount of attention in this respect because they do not sweat as much as horses in work. Furthermore, too thorough grooming of horses kept out can compromise the protective functions of the coat against bad weather conditions.

Growth promoters see **Additives**.

Gruel A traditional refreshing drink for tired horses, also used as a 'nutritional enemata' (enema). Made from oatmeal or other grains, and sometimes from boiled linseed, prepared in hot water and allowed to cool before use. Occasionally a small quantity of spirit (whisky) or a pint of ale would be added if the horse was very tired. See **Enema**.

Grunting Also known as Bulling. A traditional attempt at testing for respiratory soundness.The horse was either threatened with a stick, or 'dug' in the ribs with a closed fist, whilst being held by the head against a wall. If the horse remained silent, he was presumed sound; if he grunted in fright at the stick ('grunting to the stick'), he was presumed to be of 'faulty wind'. Prospective purchasers would reject 'grunters' as they were thought likely to develop the condition known as roaring (whistling), although there is no constant correlation between the two. See also **Roaring and whistling**.

Guaiacum gum A gum resin obtained from a tropical genus of trees of the bean-caper family. Formerly used in remedies to promote secretion of the lungs and skin.

Gum ammoniacum A gum resin obtained from a Persian umbelliferous plant (Dorema) Formerly used in expectorant remedies.

Gum arabic A gum obtained from a plant of the genus *Acacia*. Traditionally used as a demulcent for coughs and sore throats, also in cases of irritation of the stomach and intestines.

Gum benjamin see **Benzoin**.

Gum tragacanth A gum resin obtained from shrubs of the genus *Astragalus*. Formerly used in cordials, and regarded as a good tonic.

Gutta percha A substance similar to rubber but harder and less flexible, obtained from Malaysian trees of the family *Sapotaceae*. Formerly used in dental work as a stopping in cases where the interdental spaces were large and allowed food to accumulate, or to fill a gap left where a tooth had been extracted.

Haem- Prefix denoting blood (haema, haemo, haemat).

Haemoglobin A substance contained in the red blood cells which is responsible for their colouration.

Haemostatic A substance that stops bleeding (haemorrhage).

Hahnemann, Samuel Christian see **Homoeopathy**.

Hamamelis virginiana see **Witch hazel**.

Hand The standard unit of measurement for the height of a horse, measured at the withers. A hand is 4 inches (10.16 cm).

Hard feed see **Concentrate**.

Harpagophytum procumbens see **Devil's claw**.

Hart's horn The antler of the red deer, used in traditional remedies either as 'shavings' or as a decoction known as 'spirit of hart's horn'. Bone and ivory shavings were also used, although the purpose of all these materials is unclear.

I▶ **Hawthorn** *(Crataegus monogyna)* A shrub or small tree found in woodland, scrub, and hedgerows throughout Europe and north Africa. Used in herbal medicine to treat conditions of the heart and circulatory system, often in conjunction with digitalis therapy. Hawthorn contains flavonoids which dilate the coronary and peripheral arteries and procyanides, which appear to slow the heart beat. The plant is unusual in that it can be used both to lower blood pressure and to restore low blood pressure to normal.

Hay Dried grass, which is usually divided into two types; meadow hay and seed hay. Meadow hay is cut from established pasture, which may have been grazed at some time or other. Seed hay is cut from pastures which have been specifically sown for hay-making; it is higher in protein than meadow hay. The quality of hay depends on five factors; the grasses and herbage of which it is composed; the soil on which it has been grown; the time at which the grass has been cut; the hay- making process; the conditions of storage. Inevitably, if fertiliser is used on the ground, this will affect the hay. Chemicals used on the pasture itself may also appear on the hay. See also **Meadow**.

Hay tea A traditional drink for recuperating horses. It is made by pouring boiling water over best-quality meadow hay; straining off the liquor, and allowing it to cool to blood heat before giving it to the horse.'

Heat see **Oestrus**.

Health The word is derived from a Germanic word meaning 'wholeness'. Good health may be discerned from the following indicators: clear eye; brightness of manner; fair or good condition and fluidity of movement; normal, easy posture; normal appetite, respiration, pulse, and temperature; regular functioning of the organs of digestion, secretion, and excretion.

Signs of poor health include: poor appetite; dry or 'staring' coat; dullness or undue excitement; uneasy or tense posture; increase, decrease, irregularity or cessation of any of the normal functions.

Heating (of food) Heating, or uncontrollable energy, is often seen as a direct result of feeding. There is no doubt that some foods do cause the horse to become more energetic than others — oats, among other foodstuffs, have been linked to exessive energy. However, heating may also be the direct result of using inappropriate raw materials in feedstuffs, such as sugars in the form of molasses.

Heaves see **Small airway disease.**

Hiera picra A traditonal remedy, containing aloes, winter's bark, snakeroot and ginger, for the treatment of intestinal disorders. Also used as a tonic.

Hellebore *(Helleborus)* A plant of which there are several species: confusion often arises over the use of their common names. The species native to Britain are *Helleborus foetidus* and *Helleborus viridis*, which are restricted to calcareous soils. There are also cultivated hybrids grown in gardens throughout the country. Hellebore has been used in medicine for various purposes: as a purgative, as a local anaesthetic, as an abortive and as an anti-parasitic. It is also a useful homoeopathic medicine, particularly for cases of head injury. It is listed as a poisonous plant — see **Poisonous plants.**

Helminths Any of the parasitic worms.

Hemiplegia Paralysis of one side of the body.

I ▶ **Hemlock** *(Conium maculatum)* An erect, branched biennial plant reaching 2m or more in height, which grows in ditches, on roadsides and waste ground. It is common in Europe, except western and central Scotland, and is also found in Asia. Formerly used in herbal medicine to treat neurological disorders, it is sedative and anaesthetic. It is also highly toxic (see **Poisonous plants**), and was used by the Ancient Greeks as a form of execution — most notably of the philosopher, Socrates. Hemlock should be treated with caution as it is easily confused with other harmless umbellifers. In homoeopathic form it is safe, and it is used to treat disorders such as leg weakness.

Hemp See **Indian hemp**.

Henbane (*Hyoscyamus niger*) An annual or biennial plant that grows to about 80cm high. It prefers waste ground, old buildings, coastal sand or shingle and is found in Europe, Asia and north Africa. It was formerly cultivated in Britain for its medicinal properties, but is now rare. Traditionally used as a sedative and painkiller; it is toxic and is listed as poisonous plant — see **Poisonous plants**. It is used safely in homoeopathy.

Herbal medicine The medicinal use of (usually unprocessed) plant material. Herbal medicine has its origins in antiquity (see **Hippocrates**, **Elbers Papyrus**). Prior to the 1940s, herbal medications were listed alongside chemical drugs and, even today, a large percentage of the thousands of drugs in common use are either derived from plants or contain chemical imitations of plant compounds. Herbal medicines can be an effective alternative to technological medicines, and are generally without the risk of side-effects if prescribed by competent individuals. Note, however, that there is no recognised qualification in veterinary herbal medicine and it is illegal for those who are not veterinary surgeons to diagnose and treat sick animals. The BAHNM maintains a register of suitably qualified and experienced practitioners of holistic therapies.

Herb Paris (*Paris quadrifolia*) A hairless perennial plant, growing to a height of some 40cm. Found throughout much of Asia and Europe; native to Britain but local in distribution, it prefers woodland and damp, calcareous soil. It is used in homoeopathy to treat problems of the nervous system. The plant itself is toxic and is listed as poisonous (see **Poisonous plants**), although its bitter taste would serve to discourage consumption in normal circumstances.

Herbs Strictly speaking, a plant with no woody stem above ground, although herbal medicine involves the use of products from other plants, including shrubs and trees.

For information on an individual herb, see entry under common name. For information on herbs that are beneficial to the grazing horse see **Meadow**. For poisonous varieties see **Poisonous plants**.

Heroic Describes the employment of medicines or measures which are dramatic and not without risk.

High-blowing Also known as trumpeting. A noise produced by air vibrating in the false nostril when the horse is first given exercise. It usually subsides as the exercise continues.

Hindgut The back part of the gut which includes the large intestine (where the bulk of the horse's food is digested).

Hinny The offspring of a stallion and a female ass.

Hippocrates A Greek physician who lived c. 460−380 BC. Hippocrates was opposed to the considerable amounts of magic which were associated with the medicine of his time, maintaining that health depended on a delicate balance of the four 'body humours'. He believed that an imbalance of these caused disease. These beliefs were widely held until the sixteenth century, but later physicians failed to appreciate Hippocrates' major contribution to medicine, which was to expound the principle that careful diagnosis was as important as prescribing. Hippocrates preferred to allow the patient to recover naturally with minimum intervention, and he appreciated the importance of the condition of the whole being, as opposed to being concerned only with a particular set of symptoms.

Hippuris vulgaris see **Mare's tail**.

Histamine A compound that is found in nearly all the tissues of the body. It causes dilation of the blood vessels and contraction of smooth muscle. It is produced in large amounts as a mediator after skin damage, and is also released in allergic reactions.

Hobbles Devices used for casting and securing horses on the ground for the purpose of examination, operation, etc.

Hogs' lard The rendered fat of the pig. Formerly used as the basis for almost all ointments; superseded by lanolin and Vaseline.

Holism A concept based on a fundamental principle of Nature — the creation and maintenance of wholes, or complete biological systems. Disharmony of any part of the system, no matter how small, has the potential to disrupt the integrity of the whole. The theory can be demonstrated in all matter, operating at all levels, from the atom and simple cell to the most complicated biological system. An example of the principle of holism can be seen in the immensely complex organisation and behaviour of individual biological cells, functioning for the good of the whole being.

Jan Christian Smutts (1870–1950) first enabled this theory to be understood in modern scientific terms and coined the phrase 'holism', which today is also used in many areas outside the natural sciences to mean generally taking account of the whole. The term has a specific technical meaning when applied to medicines and feedstuffs. See **BAHNM**, **Holistic feeding stuffs and supplements**.

Holistic feeding stuffs and supplements Those licensed under the BAHNM regulations. Such products involve the use of raw materials that are compatible with the evolved physiology of the species. For example, products for horses must not contain animal or fish derivatives, synthetic forms of vitamins, preservatives, flavourings or colourants. The product should also be of a viable holistic nutritional profile. The formulation of such products requires expertise in nutritional, veterinary and botanical science. The licensing procedure takes into account safety, efficacy, quality and nutritional viability. Licensed products carry a symbol on all packaging together with a licence number beginning HPL. See **BAHNM**, **Holism**, **Medicines Acts**, **Nutritionist**, **Borderline nutrition**.

Holistic saddles and registered holistic saddle fitters
Holistic saddles are manufactured to a BAHNM quality standard. They incorporate specific design features which enable them to be fitted in a way that is not only relevant to the horse's conformation in relation to the work expected, but also takes account of any history that may predispose saddle-related problems. It is important that such saddles are fitted by a properly trained individual and registered holistic saddle fitters are fully trained under the BAHNM scheme.

Holistic therapy Holistic therapies follow the principle of holism in that the patient is treated as a 'whole', as opposed to therapies which concentrate on treating the diagnosed disease. Holistic therapies are often regarded by the modern medical establishment as 'alternative' or 'complementary'.

Holistic therapies are often more effective than modern medicine, and have restored many patients to health when conventional methods have failed. The reason for this is that the patient is treated as a whole entity, rather than as a set of symptoms, and the treatments stimulate the body's own healing powers rather than ignoring them.

An increasing number of holistic therapies are being used by veterinary surgeons. Those most commonly employed at present are homoeopathy, herbal medicine, aromatherapy, acupuncture, shiatsu, radionics, flower remedies (Bach), osteopathy, chiropractic and holistic nutrition. There are many more which could potentially be used. See also **Alternative medicines**, **Complementary medicine**, **Traditional medicine**.

NB. Despite the fact that it is illegal for any person who

is not a veterinary surgeon to treat sick animals, an increasing number of unqualified people are offering their services in the diagnosis and treatment of disease. Apart from the legal aspects, their activities may represent a health risk. The BAHNM maintains a register of suitably qualified and experienced practitioners.

Homo- Prefix denoting similarity (from Greek *homos* = same).

Homoeopathy The system of treating disease by using highly diluted substances which are able to excite symptoms similar to the disease itself if they are given to a healthy body. The discoverer of homoeopathy was Samuel Christian Hahnemann (1755–1843), a doctor who was struck by the fact that the symptoms produced by quinine on a healthy body (his own) were similar to the symptoms of the disease it was used to alleviate (malarial disease). From this he formulated the principle '*similia similibus curentur*' (let like be cured by like). He published this theory in a scientific paper in 1796.

Hahnemann took his research further and expounded the principle of potentisation. This is based on the discovery that the medicinal power of the remedy is *increased* in proportion to its dilution. Some of the highest dilutions contain the original material at a sub-molecular level, which leads conventionally educated medical scientists to doubt the credibility of the concept. What Hahnemann had discovered was that the energy 'pattern' left by the original substance has the potential to affect the physiology of the body.

Hahnemann's methods were very successful. In 1821, during the closing stages of the battle of Leipzig, there was an epidemic of typhus. He treated 180 cases and only 2 patients died. During a cholera outbreak in 1831 a disciple of his treated 154 cases and only 6 died, while of the 1500 cases treated by conventional methods, 821 died.

This sophisticated form of medicine is a safe and effective alternative to modern therapies which involve the use of technological drugs. There are several thousand homoeopathic remedies available to the practitioner. Many of these are toxic in their original form but, because of the extreme dilutions normally used in homoeopathy, they are safe as homoeopathic remedies. However, homoeopathy should only be prescribed by veterinarians. See also **British Association of Homoeopathic Veterinary Surgeons (BAHVS)**, **Faculty of Homoeopathy**.

Homoeostasis The physiological process which maintains within certain limits the balance of the internal systems of the body, different from and despite changes in the external environment.

Honey When mixed with linseed, a traditional remedy for coughs, and often an ingredient of horse balls. Used as a nutritious laxative when mixed with gruel, and often as an ingredient of wound ointments.

I▶ **Hops** *(Humulus lupulus)* A climbing perennial plant, which naturally prefers woodland near rivers and scrubland. Found throughout most of Europe, northern Asia and North America, and widely cultivated as a flavouring for beer. An exellent appetite stimulant and traditionally used for its sedative action on the nervous system. Used in herbal medicine as a visceral antispasmodic and bitter tonic.Useful in the treatment of convalescent horses, for example after illnesses such as equine influenza, or for problems such as excitability or nervousness.

Horehound *(Marrubium vulgare)* A perennial plant preferring footpaths, waste ground and grassland, found in south and central Europe. Traditionally used to treat coughs and respiratory problems,being given either in powder form or as a decoction.

Hormone balancer The term used in herbal medicine to describe a remedy which rebalances the hormonal sysem.

Hormones Substances produced in the ovaries, testicles,

thyroid and parathyroid glands, adrenal pituitary body, etc. which, when released into the bloodstream, affect other organs and tissues.

Horse balls A compound of medicinal substances mixed with butter or other glutinous material, formed into 'balls' about the size of a pullet's egg, and administered by mouth — see **Balling iron**, **Balling gun**.

Horse doctor see **Farrier**.

Horseradish (*Armoracia rusticana*) A perennial plant preferring waste ground, fields, and watercourses; also cultivated. Common in Britain and throughout Europe. Used as a herbal antibiotic and expectorant, also for poultices in the treatment of rheumatism.

Horsetail (*Equisetum arvense*) A plant with vegetative stems up to 80cm. tall. Prefers damp, grassy sites and found throughout Europe, Asia and North America. Used in medicine to treat kidney and bladder disorders, and also for eczema and arthritis. Horsetail is toxic, containing a substance which destroys thiamine (vitamin B1), and is listed as a poison — see **Poisonous plants**.

Horse whisperer A person who uses telepathy as a means of training. See **Telepathy**.

Humulus lupulus see **Hops**.

Hydrochloric acid A chemical preparation formerly used in the treatment of digestive disorders and as a tonic and astringent.

Hydroponic grass Made by germinating barley seeds in a controlled environment. The 'grass' is harvested at about six days old and produces a feed which has an energy value roughly the same as spring grass.

Hygiene The practice of preserving good health through sanitary principles. It is often overlooked that many of the greatest advances in the control of infectious diseases have not been the development of medicines to fight them, but improvements in sanitation and nutrition, which prevent them from developing. See **Natural medicines**.

Hyoscyamus niger see **Henbane**.

Hype- Prefix denoting excess.

Hypericum see **St John's Wort**.

Hypnotic The name given to a substance that induces sleep.

Hypo- Prefix denoting insufficiency.

Hypodermic Beneath the skin. The term is usually applied to the type of syringe used for injecting drugs or other substances, or for removing fluids from the body. See **Injections**, **Needle**.

Hypoglycaemic In herbal medicine, a remedy that reduces blood sugar.

Hypotensive In herbal medicine, a remedy that reduces blood pressure.

-iasis Suffix denoting a diseased condition.

-id Suffix denoting a relationship or resemblance to something else.

Immune enhancer A term used in herbal medicine to describe a remedy that enhances the immune sysem.

Immune system The body's ability to resist infection by means of specific antibodies and circulating white blood cells

(However, the functioning of the immune system as a whole is far more complex than the work of these agents alone.) The efficiency of the immune system can be compromised by factors such as poor or inappropriate diet, stress, etc, and this increases susceptibility to disease.

Incubation period The period that elapses between the time of infection and the appearance of the symptoms of a disease. Several factors may cause variations in the incubation period of any specific disease.

Indian hemp *(Cannabis sativa)* A plant of the mulberry family, originating in central Asia. Contains substances which have a powerful effect of the nervous system, and is traditionally used to deaden pain and induce sleep. The fibrous parts of the plant were used until recently in the manufacture of rope.

Indication A strong reason for believing that a particular action or therapy is appropriate. Compare contra-indication.

Indigestion Disrupted digestion, a common cause being inappropriate ingredients in feedstuffs. Compare **Digestion**, see **Holistic feeding stuffs and supplements**.

Induration Hardening of the tissues (often with swelling).

Infection Invasion of the body by harmful organisms, such as bacteria or viruses. Typical ways by which infections are spread are: direct physical contact; by airborne droplets; by animal or insect vectors; by contaminated food or drink.

Inferior In anatomy, refers to an organ or part situated lower in the body than another point of reference — compare **Superior**.

Inflammation A response of the body to physical injury, causing swelling, pain and stiffness to the affected part.

Infusion The pouring of water over a substance in order to extract its active qualities. In herbal medicine infusions are made by taking the stems, flowers, and leaves of plants and pouring boiling water over them. They are then left to infuse until cool enough to drink. Many remedies may be given this way, provided they are palatable. For example, see **Hay tea**.

Ingestion The process by which food is taken into the body.

Inhalation The act of breathing air into the lungs — compare **Exhalation**.

Inhalations A term used in herbal medicine to describe the administration of remedies via the respiratory system. The vapours of infusions or decoctions may be inhaled.

Injection The introduction of drugs or other substances into the body by hypodermic syringe or sometimes by other means. Common routes for injection are into the skin (intracutaneous or intradermal), below the skin (subcutaneous), into a muscle (intramuscular), and into a vein (intravenous). Other routes include the abdominal cavity (intraperitoneal) and the spine (epidural). See also **Hypodermic**, **Enema**.

Innocuous Harmless.

Insecticide A substance that kills insects. Modern pharmaceutical insecticides used for the destruction of skin parasites are very effective but may have an undesirable effect on the horse. Herbal insecticidal products are an effective alternative when used in conjunction with efficient grooming and holistic nutrition — see **Pyrethrum**.

Instinct The natural impulse; that which does not require apparent thought. Instinctive actions/reactions encompass a complex co-ordination of reflexes, and are characteristic to individuals of the same species.

International unit A unit of measure commonly used in the animal feed industry to indicate the amount of artificial vitamins which have been added to the product — see **Vitamins**.

Intestinal flora The bacterial population of the gut which digest the bulk of the horse's natural diet, i.e. grass and fibrous herbage. The nutrition that the horse derives from the food depends closely upon the composition of the gut flora. Dramatic changes in the population, associated with either a change in diet, or the long-term use of inappropriate ingredients, can lead to food allergy or acute poisoning. It can also cause serious problems such as laminitis and colic. Longer-term problems associated with a disturbed gut flora are poor stamina, unthriftiness, or an unbalanced immune system. See **Immune system**, **Holistic feeding stuffs and supplements**, **Molasses**.

Intestinal parasites see **Worms**.

Intra- Prefix denoting inside or within.

Intravenous Into or within a vein. See **Injection**.

Intro- Prefix denoting in; into.

Inula helenium see **Elecampane**.

Inverted nutrition The modern trend of formulating feed-stuffs using raw materials, often by-products, which do not satisfy the nutritional requirements of the species. Such feedstuffs must then be fortified (i.e. fortification becomes the norm). See **Non-constituent ingredients**; **Borderline nutrition.**

In vitro Latin: A biological process which is made to take place outside the body, for example in a laboratory test tube. Compare ***in vivo***.

In vivo Latin: A biological process which happens within living organisms (the body). Compare **in vitro**.

Involuntary muscles Those muscles which are not under conscious control, e.g. those associated with respiration, digestion, etc Compare **Voluntary muscles**.

Iodide of mercury A chemical preparation formerly used as a counter-irritant and vessicant. Also used in diluted form for the treatment of glandular, and other, swellings.

Iodide of potassium A chemical preparation formerly used in the treatment of tumours, splints, ringbone, etc. Also used in the treatment of chronic rheumatism, and as a diuretic.

Iodide of sulphur A chemical preparation formerly used as a dressing for chronic skin eruptions.

Iodine A trace element available in the horse's natural diet, quantities varying amongst individual foods; associated with various metabolic processes. Iodine is also used as an antiseptic. – see **Iodoform**.

Iodoform A lemon-yellow crystalline compound of iodine, used as an antiseptic.

Ipecacuanha An extract from Brazilian plants of the family *Rubiaceae*. Traditionally used as an expectorant, and a valuable remedy in homoeopathy.

I ▶ **Iris** A plant of which there are two types found commonly in Britain, the yellow flag *(Iris pseudacorus)*, and the stinking iris *(Iris foetidissima)*. The former is found in marshes and wet ground, and the later in hedgerows, woodland, and on sea cliffs. Irises are poisonous, causing irritation of the stomach and intestines and elevation of body temperature. See **Poisonous plants.**

Iron A trace element available in the horse's natural diet, quantities varying amongst individual foods. Iron is indispensable as a constituent of haemoglobin, which transports oxygen from the lungs to every part of the living body. See also **Mineral**.

Isch- Prefix denoting suppression or deficiency.

Iso- Prefix denoting equality, uniformity.

Isopathy Treatment of the disease by the identical agent of the disease. Vaccination has similarities. See also **Nosode**.

-itis Suffix denoting inflammation of an organ or tissue.

Jaborandi A substance obtained from the leaves of a Brazilian rutaceous shrub *(Pilocarpus)* and from certain other sources. Traditionally used for its diaphoretic properties, and for the treatment of bronchial and abdominal problems.

Jalap An extract of the root of the *Ipomoea* or *Exogonium* plants, originally brought from Mexico. Traditionally used as a purgative medicine, usually administered in horse balls.

Jateorhiza palmata see **Calumba**.

Java pepper see **Cubebs**.

Joint The point at which two or more bones meet and are connected.

Joint evil/joint ill Infective arthritis caused by a bacterial infection which enters the body via the navel. It may be seen in foals up to the first six months of life. Strict cleanliness during foaling is an essential factor in the prevention of the condition.

Joule see **Megajoule**.

105

I ▶ **Juniper** *(Juniperus communis)* An evergreen shrub or small tree that grows in both lowland and mountainous areas of Europe, northern Asia and North America. The oil is traditionally used in horse balls as a stomachic and diuretic; also used externally in embrocations.

Juniperus sabina see **Savine**.

Kale see **Brassicas**.

Kaolin Powdered white china clay; used in poultices and for the treatment of intestinal disorders.

I ▶ **Kelp** The name used for many types of seaweed, especially the species *Ascophylum nodosum*, which grows in abundance on the west-facing coasts of Europe, as well as in the North Temperate Zones on both the Atlantic and Pacific coasts of North America. The plant is an excellent source of many nutrients, which it takes up from sea water during feeding. It is harvested commercially and used in the production of nutritional, agricultural and medicinal substances.

Kino An astringent extract from various West African trees. Traditionally used as a remedy for diarrhoea.

Labile Unstable. The term used to describe substances that readily undergo change when subjected to heat, etc.

I ▶ **Laburnum** *(Laburnum anagyroides)* Other common names: Golden Chain, Golden Rain. A tree growing 7—9m high, found as an ornamental species in gardens throughout Britain. It does not grow wild in Britain, except an escapee from cultivation. Laburnham is toxic, especially the bark and seeds, and it is a common cause of serious or fatal poisoning in horses It is listed as a poison — see **Poisonous plants**.

Lactation The yielding of milk by the mother to the foal;

the period of suckling. See also **Colostrum**.

Lactoflavin see **Riboflavin**.

Lameness A change in the natural movement of the horse which reflects pain, inability to move correctly, or weakness. Lameness may be intermittent or continuous and is governed a great deal by the speed of movement of the horse; for example a horse may walk sound and trot lame. In some cases the lameness may become eased during exercise, only to return when the horse is rested. Proper attention to correct saddling, bitting, shoeing, riding, etc. are important preventative measures.

Lamina (plural: laminae) A thin membrane or layer of tissue. In the horse, refers especially to internal structures of the foot — see **Laminitis**.

Laminitis Old names include founder, fever in the feet. Inflammation of the laminae, a layer of connective tissue contained within the hoof. The condition causes lameness because of the reluctance of the animal to put weight on the affected feet. Mechanical damage can ensue. Laminitis is often associated with overweight ponies, but is by no means restricted to such animals. There are many predisposing factors to the condition, such as unsuitable diet, hormonal problems, circulatory problems, mechanical damage, etc. It should always be viewed as a serious condition, requiring veterinary supervision. Severe laminitis may be labelled incurable, however holistic therapies are often sucessful where others have failed.

Lanolin A fatty substance, obtained from sheep's wool, used as a base for ointments and as an emollient. Although it is a natural substance, its wholesomeness now depends upon the type of sheep dip used prior to shearing, and the extent to which it is used. See also **Goose grease**, **Hog's lard**.

Lard see **Hog's lard**.

Larkspur *(Delphinium spp.)* Plant species (not native), of which a considerable variety of sizes and forms are cultivated throughout Britain. Commonly known by the generic Latin name, Delphinium. The elongated spur on the (usually blue) flowers is a distinguishing feature. All species are poisonous, but it is unlikely that animals will be poisoned by the plant unless they have access to gardens, or to garden rubbish containing it. Listed as a poison — see **Poisonous plants**.

Laryng (laryngo) Prefix denoting the larynx.

Laser therapy Laser light can be a very beneficial healing influence and stimulus. Usually, light of about 660nm (red) is used on superficial injuries, and light of about 850nm on deeper injuries to tendons, joint capsules, etc. The latter is also useful for the stimulation of acupuncture points. The frequency of laser therapy instruments should be adjusted to suit the individual case, so only properly experienced persons should use them.

Lateral Situated at, or relating to the side of, an organ or organism. Also, in anatomy, relating to the region or parts of the body that are furthest from the median (middle) plane. In radiology, the sagittal plane (a line which runs from the front of the chest to the backbone, extending the full length of the body as if dividing it into two symmetrical halves).

Laudanum A drug made from macerated raw opium, which was formerly used extensively for its narcotic, analgesic, and other properties. See **Paracelsus**.

Laurel *(Laurus nobilis)* see **Bay**.

Laxative A substance used to stimulate or increase the frequency of bowel evacuation.

Lead A heavy metal element formerly used in astringent lotions for conditions of the skin, such as mud fever. Also administered internally for conditions involving the stomach and bowel, and given in conjunction with opium to arrest haemorrhage. It is readily taken up by the tissues and can lead to poisoning in some circumstances, its effects being cumulative.

Lead plaster see **Diachylon**.

Legume Certain plants known as legumes have a higher level of protein than most types of grasses. Common types of legume are clover and sainfoin. The most popular legume for feeding to horses is alfalfa — see **Alfalfa**.

Lesion An area of tissue, damaged by disease or injury, with consequentially impaired function.

Lethargy Mental and physical sluggishness.

Ley Arable land under pasture.

Lice Small, wingless, parasitic insects of which there are two types; sucking lice and biting lice. Only one species of sucking louse, *Haematopinus asini*, is found on the horse. There are two species of biting lice which affect horses, *Damalinia equi* and *Damalinia pilosis*. Lice cause itching and loss of condition. See also **Parasite**.

Licorice *(Glycyrrhiza glabra)* A perennial plant which prefers open fields not far from running water. A native of south-eastern Europe and south-western Asia, formerly cultivated commercially in northern England.
   Licorice is widely used in herbal remedies: it has the ability to harmonise with many other herbs, and its taste is not unpleasant to most horses. Of itself, it is a valuable medicine, used mainly for digestive and respiratory problems and also helpful for a horse coming off prolonged steroid or

phenylbutazone treatment. It should be borne in mind that licorice has been linked to a rise in blood pressure in some circumstances.

Life expectancy See **Age**.

Ligament Tough, fibrous tissue that links bone to bone at a joint, holding structures together. Ligaments have some degree of elasticity and they strengthen the joint, limiting its movement in certain directions. Compare **Tendons**.

Lily of the valley *(Convalleria majalis)* A small perennial plant with white, bell-shaped flowers which appear in the spring. Native to Britain and widely cultivated. The plant contains glycosides, which make it potentially poisonous. Although there are few reports to substantiate poisoning, it is listed as a poison — see **Poisonous plants**.

Lime water An aqueous solution of calcium hydroxide. Traditionally used as an astringent in the treatment of diarrhoea, and also as an antidote to some poisons.

Linament A thin ointment that is rubbed onto the skin or applied on a dressing.

Linctus A syrup-like medicine, particularly one used in the treatment of irritating coughs.

Linseed *(Linum usitatissimum)* The seed of the flax plant. Flax was formerly cultivated in Britain for its seed and also its fibrous stem. Linseed can be used medicinally in the treatment of chronic or acute constipation. When mixed with slippery elm powder, it also makes an excellent poultice for burns. It was traditionally used as an alterative for unthrifty horses; and given with other herbs after illnesses such as influenza or strangles.

Linseed may be used in home-prepared rations to provide protein and oils to supplement a horse's diet and improve the coat. However, it MUST be cooked thoroughly before use as a feed in order to destroy an enzyme that ultimately produces the poison, cyanide. (Cover with cold water and soak for 24 hours to soften. Change the water, bring to the boil and simmer until all the seed has split) Linseed is listed as a poison — see **Poisonous plants**.

Lipoma A benign fatty tumour.

Liquor arsenicalis see **Arsenious oxide, Fowler's solution**.

Lister, Joseph see **Phenol**.

Lithothamnium calcareum see **Calcified seaweed**.

Litre A unit of volume equal to the volume of a kilogram of pure water at 4 degrees C and at a standard atmospheric pressure of 760 mmHg.

Lolium temulentum see **Darnel**.

Lolium perenne see **Ryegrass**.

Lotion A medicinal liquid preparation for external application, usually have a soothing, cooling or antiseptic action.

Lucerne see **Alfalfa**.

Lupin *(Lupinus spp.)* Lupins are perennial plants reaching 1m in height. Although not a native species, many varieties are cultivated throughout Britain. The so-called bitter varieties contain at least five toxic alkaloids, and they are listed as poisonous — see **Poisonous plants**.

Lymph A colourless fluid which circulates through the lymphatic spaces within the body. Lymph bathes the tissues, nourishes them and returns waste products from them back to the bloodstream. Certain tissues, such as cartilage and the cornea of the eye, are not provided with a blood supply at all and, for them, lymph is the only medium supplying nourishment.

Lymphatic Refers to a lymphatic vessel, or to something relating to the transportation of lymph. In herbal medicine the word is used to describe a remedy which helps the tissue-cleansing action of the lymphatic system.

Lymphatic system The network of vessels that convey lymph around the body.

Lysine An amino acid — see **Amino acids**.

Lysol A traditional antiseptic derivative of coal-tar. Formerly used in the treatment of skin wounds and for syringing out cavities of the body such as the vagina, external ear, etc. Lysol was particularly highly valued because its slightly sticky consistency meant that it stuck to the tissues, prolonging its activity.

Macro- Prefix denoting large. Compare **Micro-**.

Macro-nutrients Carbohydrates, fats and protein. Compare **Micro-nutrients**, see **Nutrient**.

Macroscopic Visible to the naked eye. Compare **Microscopic**.

Madder *(Rubia tinctorium)* A plant formerly used for the treatment of jaundice.

Magnesium A mineral that takes its name from the Greek city Magnesia, where there are large deposits of magnesium carbonate. It is present in small amounts as an integral part of many natural feedstuffs, quantities vary amongst different types. It is associated with activating a number of metabolic pathways in the body. See also **Mineral**.

Magnesium sulphate see **Epsom salts**.

Magnet therapy The application of magnetic fields to an injury site beneficially affects the blood flow, which is vital to proper healing. Optimum blood flow removes toxins from the affected area, and supplies vital nutrients and oxygen to the damaged tissue. Magnet therapy is a very old technique, in which interest was revived in Japan during the 1950s. Subsequently, it has been used successfully in the treatment of non-union fractures for over thirty years, and some 4,000 medical and scientific papers have been published on the technique. When used as part of a holistic approach to medicine, magnet therapy can be very effective. It is not a system of medicine in its own right.

Maize *(Zea mays)* A staple cereal, known as corn in the USA, that has a reputation for being heating. Like other grains, it may be fed whole to horses with good teeth. When supplied as part of a compound feed, it is normally steamed and rolled. It is a good conditioning feed and can be used as a fair proportion of the concentrate ration.

Male fern *(Dryopteris filix- mas)* A plant common in woods, banks, and ditches throughout the British Isles. Also found in Europe, northern Asia, and North America. Traditionally used in remedies for intestinal parasites and for other medicinal purposes. It is very toxic, and thus dangerous in inexperienced hands.

Malignant Describes an invasive tumour. See **Cancer**, compare **Benign**.

Mallenders and sallenders Two old-fashioned term for psoriasis as it occurred in specific areas. Mallenders was the name given to the condition when it ocurred at the back of the knee, and sallenders was the name given to it when it occured in front of the hock. The latter was common in heavy horses who were out of condition. It was characterised by watery discharge and eventual hair loss, with thickening of the skin.

Mallow Any plant of the genus *Malva*, formerly used in remedies for its emollient properties.

Malnutrition An imbalance or deficiency of the nutrients required for good health. This can occur either because of insufficient food, or because that which is fed is unsuitable. See **Holistic feeding stuffs and supplements.**

Malt liquor A drink made from barley or other grain. Traditionally used as a tonic for convalescent horses.

Manganese A trace element available in the horse's natural diet, quantities varying amongst individual foodstuffs. Associated with the uptake of enzymes. See **Mineral**.

Mange A diseased condition of the skin caused by parasites (mites). There are four varieties of mange which occur in the horse: sarcoptic, psoroptic, chorioptic (or symbiotic) and demodectic. Symptoms, which vary according to the type of disease, include hair loss, intense, continuous itching and hard, folded or broken and inflamed skin.

Mangel A variety of beet, traditionally used as an admixture for feed to provide nutrients and variety to the horse's diet. It must be cooked prior to feeding.

Mare's tail *(Hippuris vulgaris)* A tall marsh plant native to the British Isles. Traditionally used in tonics.

I ▶ **Marigold** *(Calendula officinalis)* A hairy plant which has a characteristic, rather unpleasant, smell. It prefers tips and waste ground, but also widely cultivated. Marigold is useful for digestive problems, and also has important anti-fungal and antibacterial properties. It can be used in the treatment of both internal and external wounds or ulcers. Given as a feed additive in the summer months, it helps to repel insects. See also **Sulphur.**

Marjoram (*Organum vulgare*) A perennial plant preferring dry grassland, dry, open woodland, sunny wood margins and hedges. Found throughout most of Europe and Asia. The oil of the plant was traditionally used in remedies for strains and bruises.

Marrow A red or yellow substance contained in the bone cavities. Associated with the formation of red blood cells, and platelets, which are important in the arrest of bleeding.

Marrubium vulgare see **Horehound.**

Marsh mallow (*Althaea officinalis*) A perennial plant preferring damp meadows and banks, particularly near the sea. Found in central and eastern Europe, with a range north to Britain and Denmark, and also in parts of Asia. High in mucilage, the plant was traditionally used in ointments. The roots of the plant were used as sweets and were the original 'marshmallows'.

Mashes Made by pouring boiling water over bran, stirring and allowing to cool, mashes traditionally formed the principal diet of sick horses, being valued because they were easy to digest. A bran mash should have a crumbly texture, and can be mixed with cooked linseed to make it more appetising. A bran mash can be fed to a healthy horse the night before a rest day, or after hard work.

Massage The manipulation of the soft tissues of the body with the hands. Commonly used for relaxation therapy, reduction of tension and pain, etc.

Mastication The process of chewing food.

Mastitis Inflammation of the udder. A condition which

commonly occurs in the mare after foaling. In equines it is rarely associated with infection, being more commonly physiological in nature.

Materia medica A Latin term for the substances used in medicines; also used to mean the study of medicines in various forms, including pharmacognocy, pharmacy, pharmacology and therapeutics.

Meadow Traditionally, a meadow was grassland managed in a particular way to produce forage feed for the winter months. Floristically rich hay meadows were the building blocks of Old English agriculture, and had special significance for the horse. Good quality meadowland was worth up to three times the amount of other grazing, and special covenants often prevented such meadows from being ploughed up. Meadowland was often referred to as 'Doctor Green', which is an indication of the natural therapeutic action provided by the herbage in such land.

The richest meadows carried more than a hundred different species of grasses and herbage; perhaps four times the amount of that in modern grassland. This decline is largely a consequence of modern farming methods, which favour quantity rather than species diversity, and have created chemical imbalances in the soil.

Nutritional deficiencies or imbalances caused by lack of species diversity in grassland can have implications for the health of the horse. While it would be very difficult to re-create the healthier pastures of our forefathers' day, certain species of herbs may be oversown into existing grazing in order to help counteract the imbalance. Unless holistic feeds are being given, other herbage will have to be provided from an external source. If herbal supplements are being used, care must be taken to feed the right species in the right amounts. Any commercially orientated advice on this matter should be accepted with caution.

A good basic horse paddock mixture is:
Two varieties of perennial ryegrass *(Lolium perenne)*: 50%

Two varieties of creeping red fescue *(Festuca rubra)*: 25%
Crested dog's tail *(Cynosurus cristatus)*: 10%
Rough- or smooth-stalked meadow grass *(Poa trivialis* or *Poa pratensis)*: 10%
Wild white clover *(Trifolium repens)*: 5%

Other species such as timothy or cocksfoot may also be used. Dandelion, daisy, nettle, chicory, yarrow and burnet are also suitable herbs for pastures and are of potential benefit to the horse. Many others may be considered, but the type and quality of the soil affects the way in which various species will grow. See also **Optimum nutrition**, **Field**, **Holistic feeding stuffs and supplements**, **Nitrogen**.

NB The BAHNM will give information and advice on holistic pasture management.

Meadow grass Both rough-stalked meadow grass *(Poa trivialis)* and smooth-stalked meadow grass *(Poa pratensis)* are recommended for horse pastures. See **Meadow**.

Meadow saffron *(Colchicum autumnale)* Also known as autumn crocus. A hairless perennial plant growing to about 25cm in height and found in damp meadows throughout most of Europe. In Britain, it is mainly found in central England. It is used medicinally in the homoeopathic treatment of rheumatism and circulatory problems. Meadow saffron contains a toxic alkaloid, colchinine, which is particularly concentrated in the corm and the seeds, but all parts are poisonous and meadow saffron is listed as a poison — see **Poisonous plants**.

Meadowsweet *(Filipendula ulmaria)* A tall, perennial plant preferring hay meadows, river banks, ditches, etc. Found throughout most of Europe, and eastwards through to Asia. Salicylic acid, obtained from meadowsweet as well as from the willow, is the origin of aspirin, and meadoweet has valuable anti-inflammatory properties. However, the whole plant can be more safely used than the the isolated salicylates, because the tannin and mucilage act as a buffer, reducing the potential for side-effects.

Meat An old term for hard feed.

Meat and bone meal A dried meal manufactured from the unwanted meat, bone, hooves etc., of animals slaughtered for food. Although its use has fallen out of favour, mainly because of public opinion and its association with disease, meat and bone meal has been used as a constituent of compound feeds intended for horses. See **Holistic feeding stuffs and supplements**.

Medial Relating to or situated in the central region of an organ, tissue, or the body.

Median Located at or towards the plane that divides the body into right and left halves.

Medicago sativa see **Alfalfa**.

Medical radiaesthesia The word radiaesthesia means sensitivity to and detection of the radiations or vibrations which emanate from all matter. Energy radiates from the body in patterns not unlike a magnetic field, and it may be used by the practitioner in the diagnosis and treatment of disease. In order to do this the practitioner uses faculties which lie beyond the range of physical sense perception. This is similar to the methods employed by dowsers to locate hidden objects or water underground. Medical radiaesthesia has been successfully practised as a medical discipline since about 1900, and is gaining in popularity. See also **Radionics**.

Medicated Containing substances for a medicinal purpose, for example medicated soaps, shampoos, lotions, etc.

Medication A substance introduced into the body for the purpose of treating a medical condition. Also, the treatment of a patient by the use of medicines.

Medicinal A term used to describe any substance relating to the treatment or prevention of disease. Because of the association of the word with 'the practice of medicine', it is often used to lend importance in certain circumstances where it can be misleading. For example, the term 'medicinal herbs' or 'therapeutic herbs' is often seen on unlicensed products intended for a therapeutic purpose which, strictly, infringes the terms of the Medicines Acts — see **Medicines Acts**.

Medicine The science or practice of the diagnosis, treatment and prevention of disease. The word is sometimes used more specifically to indicate the science or practice of non-surgical methods of treatment, or more generally to describe a substance used for the treatment or prevention of disease, especially one taken by mouth.

Medicines Acts. Acts of Parliament which control, amongst other things, the manufacture and sale of substances intended for a therapeutic purpose. Any product sold for a 'medicinal purpose' must have marketing authorisation. In the case of animal medicines, this is obtained from the Veterinary Medicines Directorate.

Existing outdated legislation allows the legal status of certain products, such as some types of herbs, to be open to interpretation. This means that it is possible to market a product for a medicinal purpose whilst presenting it as a feeding stuff, thus escaping the strict regulatory process for medicines. This situation leaves the consumer vulnerable, because such products have not been subjected to adequate testing to ensure safety, quality and efficacy. The consumer should be aware of the pitfalls associated with the use of such products.

In general, apart from simple traditional remedies such as garlic, medicinal products should not be used unless they have been prescribed by a veterinary surgeon, or they are licensed by the VMD (in which case they will display a licence number beginning P.L. — sometimes very small), or they are licensed holistic products (in which case they will carry a symbol and licence number beginning H.P.L). See

BAHNM, Veterinary Medicines Directorate. (The BAHNM will advise consumers on the regulatory status of any commercially available products.)

Megajoule One million joules. A joule is a decimal unit of energy named after an English Physicist, James Prescott Joule (1818–1889). It is being used increasingly to replace the calorie in nutritional contexts (a calorie is equivalent to about 4 joules). The energy level of horse feed is often expressed in megajoules.

Melanoma A highly malignant tumour usually occurring in the skin. Exessive exposure to sunlight is thought to be a contributory factor. It is a common tumour in older grey horses.

Membrane A thin layer of tissue. Membranes may be found in various locations in the body, typically surrounding organs and tissue, lining cavities, etc.

Mentha piperata see **Mint**.

Menthol   A compound extracted from peppermint oil. Traditionally used for respiratory problems, in ointments and linaments, and as an antiseptic.

Menyanthes trifoliata see **Bogbean**.

Mercuric chloride see **Chloride of mercury**.

Mercury A toxic, silvery, metallic element that is liquid at room temperature, hence the old name, quicksilver. Traditionally, various preparations of mercury were used as astringents and antiseptics.

Meridians see **Acupuncture**.

Metabolism The physical changes which occur within the

body to enable it to function – especially those by which energy is made available for movement or 'work'. Metabolism involves the breakdown and building up of many complex organic substances.

Miasm A Hahnemannian philosophical term for describing an infective agent. No directly comparable definition exists in modern medical terminology. See also reference to Hahnemann in **Homoeopathy**

Micro- Prefix denoting small. Compare **Macro-**.

Micronisation A common method of cooking grains for foodstuffs by using infra-red radiation.

Micronutrients A term describing minerals and vitamins. Compare **Macronutrients**, see **Nutrient**.

Micro-organism An organism that is too small to seen with the naked eye.

Microscopic Too small to be seen without the aid of a microscope. Compare **Macroscopic**.

Milk teeth The teeth which are present at birth, or appear during the first few weeks of life. They are deciduous (shed in due course).

Mineral Literally, 'mined from the earth'. Minerals have special significance to nutrition and are classed as 'major' or 'trace' elements depending upon their concentration in the body. They are also divided into different groups, for example non-metallic and metallic elements.

Mineral licks Blocks containing minerals such as salt, which the horse can take as needed by licking them. Some of these blocks also contain a large proportion of molasses, which is undesirable.

I▶ Mint *(Mentha piperita / spicata)* A perennial plant preferring damp ground and waste land; common in Europe and America (introduced). Cultivated as a garden plant *(Mentha spicata)* and one of the most widely used herbs. Known mainly for its digestive qualities, it has an antispasmodic effect on the digestive system, and may aid the expulsion of gas from the stomach or bowel. It can be used in sensible amounts as a regular addition to feed, and is useful if a horse is prone to colic. The oil is used externally for a variety of purposes where a cooling and anaesthetic effect is required.

Modality Modification of symptoms by such influences as temperature, time, motion, weather, etc.

Molasses A thick, sticky, black liquid which is a by-product of the sugar industry. It is found in most commercial compound feeds, forage products and sugar beet. (Other sugar products are also used under different names, such as syrup.) Sugars in this form can have an undesirable effect on horses and the use of molasses is not recommended. See **Holistic feeding stuffs and supplements**.

Monday morning disease see **Azoturia**.

I▶ Monk's hood *(Aconitum napellus)* Also known as Aconite and Wolfsbane. A perennial plant growing to around 1m high, preferring high-altitude woodland, damp woods and riverbanks. Found in many parts of Europe, often in upland areas. Used in conventional medicine as a local anaesthetic and in homoeopathy for the treatment of fevers and for some heart conditions. Also used in traditional Chinese medicine for heart disease. Monk's hood contains the toxic alkaloid, aconite, and is listed as a poison. See **Poisonous Plants**.

Morbid Literally, 'of disease' (Latin, *morbus*=disease).Caused by, or indicating disease.

Morphine   The principal alkaloid of opium, with similar properties. Found only in the opium poppy *(Papover sommiferum)* − see **Poppy**.

Mother tincture   Undiluted alcoholic solution obtained from the original source material of a homoeopathic remedy. The starting point for all potencies from soluble material.

Mould   see **Fungus**.

Moxibustion   An aid to the practice of acupuncture, where the herb moxa is wrapped around the needle whilst it is in position, and ignited. The aroma from the herb plays an important part in treatment, as does the warming effect of the needle.

Mucilage   Mucilaginous substances are contained in plants such as comfrey, flax and psyllium seeds, as well as in herbs like marsh mallow and slippery elm. When mucilage is dissolved in water or body fluids, it forms a sticky, viscous gel, which may be used to soothe inflamed and irritated tissues, whilst protecting the surface of the membranes. Mucilage is also used as a mild laxative, as it absorbs water into the bowel, which bulks out and loosens faecal contents.

Mucopurulent   Mucus which contains pus.

Mucous membrane   Moist membrane which lines many cavities of the body, such as the nasal sinuses and respiratory tract. The surface of the membrane contains glands which secrete mucus.

Mud fever and rain scald   Both mud fever and rain scald are commonly associated with bacteria. Rain scald occurs usually in the winter, when warm, damp conditions of the coat enable the organisms to multiply. Raw, oozing patches appear on the surface of the skin. Crusty scabs are then produced, accompanied by the matting of adjacent hair.

Being associated with similar organisms, mud fever thrives in damp, muddy areas. A horse kept in such conditions will be susceptible to the bacteria, as the mud with which he comes into contact will abrade the surface of the skin. Mud fever mainly affects the skin on the posterior side of the limbs, but may spread up the leg from the fetlock, even reaching as far as the stifle and abdomen in severe cases.

Muscle Bundles of fibres laid against each other, which have the ability to contract. Their primary purpose is to provide movement or force to the body or the structures within it.

Musculo- Prefix denoting muscle.

Mustard The powdered seeds of various species of the genus *Brassica*; a pungent condiment. Traditionally used in medicinal plasters and also as a poultice for ulcers and cuts. Also used as an appetite stimulant, to aid digestion, and in the treatment of circulatory problems and rheumatism.See also **Brassicas**.

Mydriatic A term used to describe a substance that causes the pupil of the eye to dilate.

Myotic A term used to describe a substance that causes the pupil of the eye to contract

Myrrh The resin of *Commiphora*, a genus of plants of the family *Burseraceae*, native to tropical Asia and Africa. Formerly used as a tonic when mixed with bitters such as gentian or aloes. Also considered good for chronic coughs when mixed with opium.

Narcosis A state of unconsciousness, or diminished consciousness, ranging from sleep to deep coma. Usually caused by a drug. (From the Greek *narke*= numbness.)

Narcotic A substance which induces narcosis, used therapeutically to induce sleep or to reduce the sensation of pain.
Overdoses of narcotics can be fatal. Morphine is an example
of a natural narcotic drug — see **Poppy**.

National Research Council An independent scientific
organisation which produced what are known as the 'NRC
Figures (1989)' on the nutritional requirements of animals.
Their publication gives detailed nutrient requirements for
horses, together with recommendations on the use of by-
products and synthetic products, such as vitamins. Much of
the information given for horses is extrapolated from other
species but, despite the fact that the accuracy and relevance
of these somewhat outdated figures are now under serious
doubt, they are still commonly used by manufacturers for
formulating equine feedstuffs.

The authors themselves began by pointing out that many
questions in equine physiology had not been resolved and, in
the light of increasing feed-related health problems, it seems
that their concern was entirely justified. A passage from the
introduction reads 'The sub-committee found large gaps in
the published information, unresolved conflicting reports, and
a disconcerting need to apply information gathered under
one set of circumstances to very broad and diverse management systems'.

The publication goes on to say that horses should be
treated as individuals. Many factors should be allowed for,
such as metabolic and digestive differences between horses,
health status, variations in the nutrient availability of the
feed ingredients, and inter-relationships of nutrients.
Furthermore, there is concern over the recommendations
made about the use of synthetic vitamins because the required
levels were not (and still are not) known. The authors also
expressed concern about extrapolating recommendations for
equines from work done on other species. Compare **Holism**,
Holistic feeding stuffs and supplements.

Natural According to the established order of things,

governed by Nature and not by mankind. The word is often used in a misleading way by manufacturers of feeds and feed additives to imply that a product is something other than it is. For example, unsuitable materials, such as molasses, are often described as 'natural', a description which may be misleading because, while they may come from a natural source, they are processed in a way which makes them unnatural. Another example of this is the use of artificial vitamins, which are added to many compound horse foods to fortify either usuitable or over-processed raw materials. These are often described as 'nature identical', which is meant to convey the idea that they must qualify as being the same as natural vitamins merely because their structure appears to be the same. This reasoning is flawed, because the truly natural world contains factors vital to life which cannot necessarily be reproduced in a laboratory. For example saltwater fish will not survive in artificial seawater, despite the fact that it is chemically identical to real seawater. As another example of this, in a human study, a group of patients suffering from digestive disorders were given extra B complex vitamins from a natural source. Their distressing symptoms were alleviated or completely cured. However, when the natural vitamins were replaced with laboratory-produced ones, the symptoms returned. See also **Holistic feeding stuffs and supplements**.

Natural medicines Remedies derived from plants or other natural sources. Up until the 1940s, natural remedies such as herbs were listed alongside the modern drug equivalents, but they gradually fell into disuse. Despite the fact that a very large proportion of the new 'wonder drugs' were based either on natural materials or chemical copies of them, herbal medicine was discarded as outdated and useless. There were vested interests in propagating this myth: the pharmaceutical industry realised the financial implications of ousting traditional medicines made from plants — which cannot, of course, be patented.

There are many advantages to be derived from the use of

natural medicines as opposed to technological ones, lack of side-effects being one. It is often stated that pharmaceutical products have saved many lives, but this statement should be considered in context with other factors affecting health — for example, see **Hygiene**.

Navicular disease Navicular disease is a degeneration of the navicular bone in the foot, a bone which, in simple terms acts as a pulley, across which the deep digital flexor tendon runs. One of the consequences of navicular disease is that the surface of the bone becomes pitted, and this can interfere with the action of the tendon and cause considerable pain.

There are thought to be several factors which contribute to the condition. Among them are the conformation of the foot associated with concussion, incorrect shoeing, irregular blood supply to the area and incorrect gait caused by spinal misalignment. Holistic medicine, nutrition, and general management can be very successful in alleviating this distressing and difficult condition, returning the horse to normal work in most cases.

Neatsfoot oil An oil obtained from the hooves of cattle. A traditional leather dressing and included as an ingredient in remedies for application to the skin, presumably because of its oily properties.

Necrosis Death of tissue (adjective, necrotic).

Needle A slender, sharp-pointed instrument. Needles for medical use are generally made of steel. Hollow needles, used for injecting drugs, are usually referred to as hypodermic. Solid needles are used for suturing (stitching) tissue. Special needles, made from various materials, are used for acupuncture. See also **Acupuncture**, **Hypodermic**, **Injection**.

Neoplasia Literally, new growth. A term usually reserved for cancer.

Nerve A cord-like structure of fibres. The nervous system is a vastly complex network which carries impulses to and from all parts of the living body in order to bring about its normal functions.

Nerve block A method of rendering a part of the body insensitive by injecting an anaesthetic drug around the associated nerve. This prevents the sensation of pain from reaching the brain.

Nervine A term used in herbal medicine to describe a substance which calms the nerves.

I ▶ **Nettle** *(Urtica dioica)* A perennial plant covered with stinging hairs, preferring waste ground, woods, etc. Found in all temperate regions of the world, it is generally regarded as a weed in gardens and most farmland in Britain. Nettles, however, are a valuable addition to the daily diet of the horse, being rich in minerals, particularly iron, calcium and potassium. They are therefore recommended as a constituent of horse pasture (see **Meadow**).

Because the plant helps with the absorption of iron, it is useful in the veterinary treatment of anaemia. It has a traditional use in the treatment of skin ailments such as sweet itch, and is also used for problems where a cleansing of the system is required, since it has great eliminative properties via the liver and kidney.

Neuro- Prefix denoting nerves or the nervous system.

Neurosis A psychological state in which there is inappropriate behaviour. Symptoms may include severe emotional stress, unusual compulsive behaviour, anxiety or depression.

Niacin Vitamin B3. See **Vitamins**.

Nicking The cutting and re-organisation of the muscles of the horse's tail in order to maintain a higher tail carriage.

The practice was carried out for reasons of fashion and was made illegal in England in 1948.

Nicotiana tabacum see **Tobacco**.

Nitrate of potassium see **Saltpetre**.

Nitric acid A powerful caustic, traditionally used to remove warts and other growths from the skin. Also used for the treatment of ulcerating sores. Diluted nitric acid was mixed with hydrochloric acid and used in the treatment of liver problems. The substance is used safely in homoeopathy.

Nitrogen A gaseous element that is a major constituent of air, and an essential constituent of proteins. Nitrogen, applied to the land in the form of artificial fertilisers, is one of the major factors contributing to the herbal depletion of grassland. It is applied to encourage swift growth, and it does so very effectively, but at the expense of the slower-growing varieties, which become smothered. Its application also depletes the soil of valuable trace minerals. Farmers today are applying nitrogenous fertilisers at twenty times the rate that was used in the 1940s. Not only has this drastically reduced the number of species of flora; in some parts of the country the levels of nitrogen wash-off are becoming hazardous to health.

Nitro-glycerine Used as a drug used to dilate blood vessels. Traditionally used for heart spasm, asthma, 'broken wind' and convulsions. In poisonous doses paralysis of both motion and sensation results, death is by cessation of respiration.

Non-aerobic exercise see **Exercise**.

Non-constituent ingredients Processed or artificial ingredients that are introduced into a feedstuff or supplement in order to try to replace those which should be integral parts of the raw materials. Artificial vitamins and processed sugars, which are often used in compounded horse feeds, are non-constituent ingredients. See also **Inverted nutrition**.

Nosodes   Homoeopathic prevention of specific diseases is accomplished by the use of remedies which are prepared from diseased tissue or secretions, using the normal succussion method. The body reacts to these dilute yet potent remedies by sharpening its defence mechanisms in response to the 'challenge'. Because this method of protection is different from the orthodox method of immunisation (which involves the injection of a suspension of modified micro-organisms, often with adjuvants and other material) it is without side-effects. See **Vaccination**.

Notifiable diseases   Those diseases which must be notified to the police, or the goverment department concerned. Those affecting horses include African horse sickness, anthrax, dourine, equine contagious metritis, equine infectous anaemia, equine encephalomyelitis, epizootic lymphangitis, glanders and rabies. Mercifully, outbreaks are rare in Great Britain.

Noxious   Hurtful, not wholesome; damaging to tissues.

NRC figures   see **National Research Council.**

Nut galls   see **Oak bark.**

Nuts (horse)   see **Compound food.**

Nutrient   A substance obtained from food which is of physiological value. The term includes carbohydrates, proteins, fats, minerals, vitamins and water. Nutrients are necessary for energy, organ function, food utilisation and cell growth. See also **Micronutrients, Macronutrients.**

Nutrition   The study of food and the physiological process by which it is converted and absorbed by the body. Modern equine nutrition has its roots in agricultural science, which concerns itself with converting food to either meat or milk in the cheapest possible way. As such, it is a polarised discipline, often involving the use of by-products and other materials which are incompatible with the evolved physiological requirements of the species. Compare **Holistic feeding stuffs**, see **Inverse nutrition**.

Nutritional supplements Additives used to improve the nutritional quality of feedstuffs. The market for nutritional supplements has grown greatly over recent years, largely because of the (often correctly) perceived inadequacies of horse feeds and also to some extent because of impoverished grazing and hay. In general, supplements such as multivitamin preparations are overused. This may cause problems in some cases, because some artificial vitamins can be toxic in large doses. While the use of supplements is sometimes justifiable, those given should be from a natural source. Since most are not, their use should be carefully considered. See **Holistic feeding stuffs and supplements**, **Meadow, BAHNM**.

Nutritional therapy A therapy which seeks to change the profile of the diet gently, whilst taking into consideration current environmental, physiological and psychological factors which may affect the health of the horse. Although nutritional therapy is mainly concerned with disease prevention, it is often used both in support of, and as a part of, specific veterinary treatment. The line between nutrition and medicine is often blurred in this respect. When used as part of a holistic approach to medicine, nutritional therapy can be very effective, but it is not a system of medicine in its own right.

Nutritionist One who has studied the effect of food on the physiology of the body. Since there are no legal restrictions, anyone can style themself a nutritionist. While many nutritionists are highly qualified in specific areas, some have no relevant knowledge or qualifications in other areas. For example the term does not, of itself, imply any proper understanding of holistic principles, which embrace other disciplines such as the veterinary and botanical sciences. See also **Holism, Holistic feeding stuffs and supplements**.

Nutritive A term used in herbal medicine to describe a substance that is rich in nutrients.

Nux vomica The seeds of the East Indian tree, strychnos, the chief alkloid of which is strychnine, potentially a deadly poison. Traditionally used in the treatment of urinary and digestive problems, nux vomica also given to older stallions on commencement of the breeding season. It is a valuable homoeopathic remedy, which may be used to treat colics characterised by constipation and spasm.

Nystagmus Rhythmic, jerky movements of eyes, usually laterally and usually involuntarily.

Oak bark The oak *(Quercus spp.)* is a common tree throughout Britain. Growing in woodland, parkland and hedges, it may live to be many hundreds of years old. The bark of the young trees, and the branches, are potent sources of tannin, and the strongly astringent bark (tanner's bark) was formerly used for tanning leather. Medicinally, oak bark is most useful in the treatment of diarrhoea. The nut-galls found on many trees are also sources of tannin, and powdered nut-galls can be used in the treatment of surface tissue, where limited circulatory effect is required. Since large quantities can damage the kidneys, oak derivatives should only be used by a veterinary surgeon. Horses who ingest significant amounts of oak material usually void very dark brown urine. See **Acorns,Tannins, Tannic acid, Tannic acid jelly**.

Oats The seeds of the genus of grasses *Avena*, especially *Avena sativa*, oats are the traditional grain food for horses.

Provided the diet as a whole contains the right amount of different herbage, oats can be used as the total concentrate part of the feed. They have been associated with heating problems and, although this is not a constant finding, they must be fed with care in this respect. Naked oats are a development of the ordinary variety, which lose their husks during harvest. Because naked oats contain up to 27% more energy than ordinary oats, weight for weight, they must be fed accordingly.

Obesity A condition in which an excess of fat accumulates in the body because more food is consumed than is necessary for the exercise taken. Obesity is associated with respiratory and muscolo-skeletal problems, and also with some skin disorders.

Obstetrics The science of the care of the mother during pregnancy and foaling, and the care of the mother and foal for some weeks after the birth.

Oedema An accumulation of fluid in the tissue spaces of the body which may be local, as a result of an injury, or general. General oedema is often treated with diuretic drugs.

Oestridae see **Bot-fly**.

Oestrogen One of a group of steroid hormones, produced by the ovaries, that control sexual development and induce oestrus. Oestrogen is also found in plants.

Oestrogenic The name given to a substance (especially in herbal medicine) which resembles the actions of oestrogen.

Oestrus cycle The sexual cycle of the mare, with alternating periods of oestrus (when the mare accepts the stallion) and dioestrus (when she rejects him). Typical oestrus (also known as 'heat') lasts for 5 days; dioestrus for 15 days – although these timescales can vary.

Oil of Wintergreen see **Wintergreen oil**.

Oils and fat The term 'oils and fats' may appear in lists of ingredients of compound feeds and additives, in which they are included as an energy source. This description can be misleading because it actually covers 'oils and fats from animal or vegetable sources and their derivatives'. Most manufacturers are now listing ingredients by name, but some still do not do so. Only oils and fats from vegetable sources are suitable for horses — see **Holistic feeding stuffs and supplements.**

Oil-seed rape A popular summer farm crop in Great Britain, oil-seed rape is grown for its oil, and can be recognised by its bright yellow flowers and pungent aroma. It is a common cause of respiratory problems for horses living or exercising in the area in which it is grown.

Oils (volatile) Volatile oils from amber, aniseed, caraways, juniper, origanum, etc. were traditionally used in various remedies for external application and also as ingredients in horse balls. See also **Aromatherapy**.

Ointment A semi-solid greasy material containing one or more substances for medicinal purposes. Applied to the skin or mucous membrane.

Olfactory Pertaining to the sense of smell.

Onion *(Allium cepa)* A hairless biennial plant, originally from central Asia, widely cultivated for food use. It is rich in essential oils, also thiopropionaldehyde, which causes the eyes to water when the bulb is peeled. Onion was formerly used by horsemen to encourage an animal to stale (urinate) by placing a piece within the sheath of a male, or in the vagina of a mare. The plant is used in homoeopathy for the treatment of bronchial and intestinal problems.

Ophthalmic Concerned with the eye

Opiate One of a group of narcotic drugs obtained from opium, or a drug with opium-like qualities. Those derived from opium include apomorphine, codeine, morphine and papaverine. Opiates depress the central nervous system, relieve pain and supress coughing. Their presence may contravene the rules of equestrian sports. See **Poppy**.

Opisthotonus Describes the posture of an animal in extensor spasm; head and neck back, legs outstretched, back hollowed.

Opium see **Poppy**.

Opodeldoc The name given by the physician Paracelsus (b. 1493) to a soap linament which consisted of soft soap, camphor, alcohol and essential oils. Formerly a popular remedy for sprains and bruises.

Optic Concerning the eye or vision.

Oral Relating to the mouth.

Organ Any part of the body which consists of more than one tissue, and which has a particular function.

Organic Organic crops are those grown without the use of artificial products such as fertilisers and pesticides. Official accreditation of such crops is a function of the Soil Association, the method of production being approved as part of the Quality Standard for Holistic Feeding Stuffs and Feed Additives. see **Holistic feeding stuffs**, **Additives**.

Organotropy Affinity of a substance for a particular organ or organ system

Organum vulgare see **Marjoram**.

Orpiment Usually, arsenic trisulphide; the name formerly used for any of several remedies that included arsenic as an ingredient. See **Arsenic**.

Osmosis The automatic movement of fluid from a concentrated solution to less concentrated one, through a membrane. The membrane allows passage of the fluid, but not the substance in dilution. The fluid thus further dilutes the solution into which it has passed. Osmosis plays an important role in controlling the distribution of fluids in the body.

Osteopathy A system of treating ailments using manipulation of the body, founded by Dr Andrew Still (1828—1917). It involves rhythmic movements of massage, with low velocity and high amplitude. Both osteopathy and chiropractic are used regularly for horses, commonly for problems involving the back. Compare **Chiropractic**, see **Physiotherapy**.

Ovaries The female reproductive organs, situated in the mare's abdomen, lying a little below and behind the kidneys. Responsible for the production of ova (eggs). Each ovum is caught by its oviduct, and is either fertilised and develops, or passes through the system to be voided from the body.

I▶ **Over-reach** A wound to the heel of the forefoot, caused by the front edge of the shoe of the hind foot striking down upon it. Usually occurs during galloping or jumping, either as a result of the forelimb being insufficiently extended, or of the hind limb being over-extended. It can also occur as a result of pelvic misalignment.

Oxalic acid A very toxic acid found in many plants, such as sorrel and the leaves of the rhubarb. Oxalic acid is used in some bleaching powders.

Oxygen A colourless, odourless gas which makes up about one fifth of the atmosphere. Oxygen is essential for the functioning and survival of all living tissues; it is distributed to all parts of the body via the circulatory system.

Oxymel A mixture of vinegar and honey.

Oxymel of squills A traditional remedy used as an expectorant and as a mild laxative, containing honey and vinegar of squills. See **Squill**.

Oxytocic The name given to a substance which induces or accelerates labour.

Paddock see **Meadow**.

Pain Physical pain is an unpleasant and/or distressing sensation caused by the stimulation of sensory nerves. It is commonly a warning of bodily danger, triggering an action which should put an end to it. For example, the pain experienced as a result of a strained limb causes lameness, thus protecting the limb from further damage whilst allowing it to heal. Mental, or psychological pain can be as unpleasant as the physical variety: it may be caused by emotional disturbance and distress, which can be products of many factors.

The management of pain, in conjunction with the use of medicines and nursing practices which support the body's own healing processes, are central to proper holistic veterinary treatment.

The fact that a horse is not showing obvious signs of discomfort is not necessarily an indication that he is not in pain. For example, back injuries are often missed because the resultant behavioural problems are related to schooling deficiencies, rather than being associated with musculoskeletal malfunction or saddling problems. See also **Analgesic**, **Stress**.

Palliative A treatment which gives temporary relief to the symptoms of a disease but is not a cure.

Palpation Examination of the body by feeling with the

hands. Abnormalities associated with physical damage or disease may be detected in this way by skilled and experienced people.

Palpitation Irregular or abnormally rapid heart beats.

Panacea A cure-all; one medicine that is the answer to all ailments. Many herbal products, particularly those which have notable healing properties, such as aloe vera, are often promoted by marketeers as panaceas. While the medicinal properties of such remedies may be useful in a variety of situations, the claims made for their effectiveness are often exaggerated or distorted. In some cases they may even be entirely misplaced. This is irresponsible marketing, and is one of the reasons why natural medicines are seen in a bad light.

Pangamic acid Vitamin B15 – see **Vitamins**.

Pantothenic acid Vitamin B5 – see **Vitamins**.

Paracelsus Known as 'the father of European pharmacy and pharmaceutical chemistry', Paracelsus was born in Zurich in 1493. He trained as a physician in Italy, and was appointed professor of medicine and city physician of Basle in 1527. He is famous for his treatment of diseases, particularly syphilis, with metal salts; also for his plant remedies. His tincture of opium, which he called 'laudanum', was especially popular.

Paraffin oil An oil associated with the manufacture of paraffin, traditionally used as an insecticide. It was formerly used widely by the British abroad, for example in South Africa, to repel mosquitoes which were linked with the spread of African horse sickness, a weak solution being applied to the horse daily during troublesome periods.

Paralysis Loss of the power of movement of part of the body, caused by disorder of associated nerves or muscles. The degree of paralysis may be variable, from a slight loss of function to total immobility. It may be temporary or permanent, depending on the cause.

Paraplegia Paralysis of hind limbs.

Parasite An organism that lives on another, relying on its host for food and protection. Parasites may be internal, such as worms (endoparasites), or external, such as lice (ectoparasites). Their affect on the horse will depend upon the degree and type of infestation, varying from slight skin irritation in the case of a few lice to serious gut damage or death in the case of a heavy worm infestation.

Preventative measures, including herbal insecticidal washes and thorough grooming, can be effective in controlling ectoparasites, while holistic nutrition is an important factor in the control of endoparasites. Heavy infestations may indicate the need for dramatic action, entailing the use of some of the modern pharmaceutical products. While killing the parasites, these may have other undesirable effects upon the horse.

Parasiticide A substance that kills parasites.

Parenteral route A route of administration of a medicine other than via the alimentary canal.

Parrot-mouth A congenital defect or deformity in which the upper incisor teeth overlap the lower ones. This condition may result in serious feeding difficulties, but it can be improved with skilful dentistry.

Particulars Symptoms applying to individual organs, organ systems or parts of the body.

Parturient The name given to a substance (particularly in herbal medicine) that facilitates birth.

Parturition Birth (of a foal).

Pasteur, Louis (1822-1895) French pioneer of bacteriology, whose knowledge made it possible to formulate the germ-based theory of disease. He gave his name to the process, pasteurisation, by which infective micro-organisms in milk are destroyed by heat.

Pathogen Any agent that causes disease, especially parasitic micro-organisms such as bacteria.

Pathological Relating to or arising from disease.

Pathology The study of disease with the aim of discovering its nature and cause. See **Physiology**.

Peas Papillonious climbing plants, the seeds of which are good sources of protein and energy. They are commonly used in compound feeds.However, because peas can be heating, they should only form a very small part of the concentrate ration.

Peat moss Brown, or sometimes black, altered vegetable matter found in bogs. Formerly dried and used as stable bedding, particularly during convalescence for horses with sensitive feet.

Pedal ostitis Inflammation of the pedal bone. As with all conditions of the foot, expert farriery is essential, and proper holistic therapy, management and nutrition are usually effective.

Pellitory of Spain (*Anacylus pyrethrum*) A plant, similar to chamomile, native to northern Africa and southern Europe. The name is also commonly extended to several similar plants, such as yarrow and feverfew. Traditionally used as a digestive stimulant.

Penicillin An antibiotic drug, derived from the mould *Penicillium chrysogenum,* which is effective against infections caused by a wide variety of bacteria. Penicillin was developed from the work of the bacteriologist Alexander Fleming in 1928.

Penis The male organ through which urine and semen are discharged. During mating the penis is enlarged and becomes stiffly erect to deliver semen into the mare's reproductive tract. During urination the penis extends loosely from the prepuce, being returned by the action of the retractor muscles.

Pepper see **Capsicum**.

Percussion A diagnostic technique which reveals the presence of fluid in, or abnormal solidification or enlargement of, different organs. This is acheived by sensing the different resonances produced when the body is tapped, either with an instrument, or with the fingers.

Percussion injury An injury, usually to the leg joints, which arises from sudden hard physical force being placed upon them. Caused by actions such as jumping on hard ground.

Perineum The area around the anus or between the anus and vulva.

Peristalsis The means by which matter is moved along the intestines. It is an involuntarily process, being caused by the wave-like movement of the intestinal walls.

Permanganate of potash A chemical preparation of purple crystals which, when dissolved in water, produces an antiseptic fluid.

Persicaria bisorta see **Snakeroot**.

Peruvian Bark see **Balsams** (of Peru).

Pesticide An agent which kills insects or other harmful organisms in crops. The residues of harmful pesticides may find their way into the horse's diet.

Petroleum jelly see **Vaseline**.

pH An expression used to indicate the amount of hydrogen ions in a solution, and thus its alkalinity or acidity. A neutral solution will have a pH of 7; above 7 indicates alkalinity and below 7 indicates acidity.

Pharmaceutical Pertaining to drugs for a medicinal use. Whilst natural medicines are also drugs, the term pharmaceutical is normally used to indicate a drug that is man-made or 'artificial'.

Pharmaceutical Merchants List (Medicines) This list includes medicines, such as wormers, which are restricted by law to sale through approved outlets only. Such outlets must employ trained staff who are capable of giving advice on the use of the product. Compare **Prescription Only Medicines**.

Pharmacognosy The study of drugs derived from plants. This study can lead to the unwise practice of extracting, purifying, and concentrating so-called 'active ingredients' at the expense of the whole herb.

Pharmacology The science of the action of drugs on the body. It includes the study of the origins of drugs, their chemical structure and medicinal usage.

Pharmacopoeia A book containing a list of drugs used in medicine, including a description of their uses and actions.

Pharmacy A place where drugs are prepared.

Phenol *(carbolic acid)* A strong tar derivative used in disinfectants, and in preparations for cleansing wounds, etc.

Phenol is related to the cresols (creosote) and has similar properties, being a corrosive poison if swallowed. Natural phenolic substances have been in use ever since the Ancient Egyptians used them as embalming fluids, but it was not until after 1865 that they began to be widely used in medicine, having been introduced by Joseph Lister.

Phenylbutazone An anti-inflammatory and analgesic drug introduced in 1949, and now withdrawn from general use in human medicine, because of its potentially serious side-effects. It also counteracts the healing effects of homoeopathy and other natural healing mechanisms. Despite the possibility of side-effects in horses, and the fact that there are alternative methods of treatment, it is still widely used for problems associated with injury and arthritis. Its use is prohibited in competitive sports under Jockey Club and FEI rules.

Phlegm A commonly used non-medicinal term for sputum.

Phleum pratense see **Timothy.**

Phosphorus A major mineral which is available in the horse's natural diet, quantities varying amongst individual foods. Closely associated to calcium in bone.

Photophobia Literally, fear of light. Describes the blinking of animals when confronted with light to which they are over-sensitive.

Photosensitivity A condition in which the surface of the skin becomes sensitive to sunlight. The skin becomes reddened and inflamed and eventually the affected areas become dry and slough off. Photosensitivity occurs as a result of a combination of exposure to sunlight and some substance that has been eaten or applied to the skin. Such substances are know as photosensitizers and are thought to include various drugs, dyes or other chemicals, and plant

143

derivatives. For example, plants such as St John's Wort can, when ingested, cause the problem through dysfunction of the liver - see **St John's Wort**.

Physic A traditional term given to a remedy which produced purging of the digestive system. Horses where commonly 'physicked' when being put back onto hard feed after being out at grass. Physics were also administered as a general tonic for the digestive system.

Physical Relating to the body, rather than the mind.

Physic ball A medicinal ball - see **Horse balls**.

Physiology The study of the functioning of living organisms. Together with anatomy and pathology, physiology is the basis of medical science.

Physiotherapist A person who practises physiotherapy. Manipulative therapists are commonly consulted for problems involving the musculo-skeletal system, particularly those involving the horse's back. However, the technique should only be applied to a correctly aligned skeletal system. There are many people offering physiotherapy who have either inappropriate qualifications or none at all, and who may be incompetent. There is proper training available which enables the practitioner to work under the direction of a veterinary surgeon. Physiotherapy should be used as an adjunct to medicine, not as a substitute for it; it is not a system of medicine in its own right.

Physiotherapy The use of physical methods including heat, light, electric current, massage, manipulation and remedial exercise to promote healing. See **Chiropractic**, **Electro-therapy**, **Magnet therapy**, **Osteopathy**, **Ultrasonic therapy**.

Physostigma venenosum see **Calabar bean**.

Phyto-prevention The use of herbs in preventing disease — see **Prophylactic**.

Phytotherapy The use of plant remedies in medicine.

Pimento The dried, unripe fruits of a West Indian tree, *Pimenta officinalis*. Formerly known as Cayenne pepper, now known as allspice or Jamaica pepper. Traditionally used as a stomachic and digestive carminative, often in conjunction with capsicum — see **Capsicum**.

Pimpernel *(Anagallis arvensis)* Also known as Scarlet Pimpernel, Shepherd's Weatherglass, Poor Man's Weatherglass. A small annual or perennial plant reaching about 10cm in height, preferring cultivated ground and waste land, and found almost world-wide. The plant is used medicinally in the homoeopathic treatment of skin and liver problems. It has long been regarded as poisonous and, although its poisonous principle is uncertain, it is listed as a poisonous plant — see **Poisonous plants**.

Pimpinella anisum see **Anise**.

Placebo An inert substance such as chalk, given instead of medicine, and used in human trials for drugs. Placebos are also sometimes prescribed by doctors, as they can appear to relieve the symptoms of a disease simply because the patient believes that they will.

Critics of homoeopathy often claim that the medicines simply act as placebos. It is difficult, however, to imagine the placebo effect leading to the satisfactory cure of animals by homoeopathic medicines.

Placenta Commonly, the medical term for the afterbirth although, strictly speaking, the word means the medium by which the mother nourishes the foetus. The placenta forms a protective environment in which the foetus floats, being cushioned from shock whilst being allowed free, though limited, movement.

It is important that the placenta is completely voided from the mare after parturition. A common cause of failure of this process may be laminitis.

Plantar Relating to the sole of the foot.

Plasma The fluid in which the blood cells are suspended.

Plaster Adhesive tape used to keep dressings, etc. in place.

Plaster of Paris A preparation of calcium sulphate (originally found near Paris), which sets into a hard cast after water is added. Used to immobilise limbs.

Plasters (medicinal) Medicinal plasters, also known as charges, were once commonly used to support sprained and weakened tendons, joints, ligaments, or fractured bones. They had a base of pitch, resin, wax, or a mixture of these substances. This base was melted and the drugs to be used were mixed into it. The mixture was allowed to cool and then applied to the injured part with a spatula. Plasters would stick to the surface of the skin and stay in place for a considerable time. See **Diachylon**.

PMLs See **Pharmaceutical Merchant's List** (medicines).

Pneumonia Inflammation of the lung caused by contact with a toxic or irritant material, or to infection by any of a wide spectrum of micro-organisms.

Poa pratensis see **Smooth-stalked meadow grass**.

Poa trivialis see **Rough-stalked meadow grass**.

Poison Any substance which, in small amounts, may damage, irritate, or impair the activity of living organisms, or cause their death. Many plants which are regarded as poisonous may also be used in medicine — see **Toxins**.

Poisonous plants   Many species of plants contain substances known as toxins (Greek = poison for arrows), most of which may be classed as poisonous, but all of which have the potential to harm the body. However, substances regarded as poisonous for one species may not be so for another. This is known as 'species difference'. For example, pigs thrive on quantities of acorns which would cause poisoning in cattle. Deer are reported to be able to feed on rhododendron and yew, and grey squirrels on amanita mushrooms, all of which are fatal to other species. There are also variations within certain species: for example some types of rabbit are not adversely affected by deadly nightshade. Goats are less affected by this plant than many other animals.

In some cases, the toxicity of a plant will vary as a result of several factors, such as time of year; also certain parts of a plant may be toxic while other parts are not.In the potato for example, the stems, leaves, flowers and fruits are toxic.

Poisoning may also be a question of degree, depending upon the severity of the toxicity caused. Sometimes the effect may be so slight as to go unnoticed. Problems such as non-specific allergies, weight loss, lethargy, and mild digestive problems may not necessarily be associated with toxins, and the correct diagnosis may therefore be missed.

It is thought that, along with other grazing animals, many horses commonly suffer from the effects of mild toxicity. This may be because they are forced to feed on certain plants in the absence of more suitable species. Compound feeds containing unsuitable ingredients, such as by-products and molasses, probably contribute to the problem, along with the indiscriminate use of synthetic products and unsuitable poly-herbal feed additives.

The reason why feral horses do not usually poison themselves is probably because they have access to an abundance of natural food: many poisonous plants are unpalatable, and are usually ignored if there are other things to eat. Horse-sick, weed-infested pastures present the greatest risk to the modern horse.

The toxins of some poisonous plants, such as ragwort and bracken, build up slowly in the system and cause a gradual decline in health as they accumulate. Others, such as yew, can poison a horse immediately. Horses will rarely eat ragwort unless it is broken down and wilted, which appears to make it more attractive to them.

The plants found in the Great Britain, which are generally considered poisonous in their own right, are:

Acorn, alder buckthorn, black bryony, black nightshade, bracken, broom, buckthorn, celandine, chickweed, columbine, corn cockle, cowbane, darnel, deadly nightshade, foxglove, hellebore, hemlock, henbane, herb paris, horsetail, irises, laburnum, larkspur, lily of the valley, linseed, lupins, meadow saffron, monk's hood, pimpernel, poppies, potato, privet, ragwort, rhododendron, St John's wort, thornapple, white bryony, yew.

There are many other species of plant and shrub that may have a toxic effect depending upon the circumstances.

The most common causes of fatal or serious poisoning in horses are ragwort, yew, laburnum and bracken.

Pollen The fertilising powder found in the flowers of plants and trees. During the summer months pollens circulate in the air and are associated with respiratory problems in horses. See **Oil-seed rape.**

Poll evil An old term for an infected swelling on one or both sides of the neck below the poll. Usually caused by mechanical damage, such as striking the head on a low doorway. The resultant infection usually requires attention by a veterinary surgeon.

Polychrest One of the deep-acting, extensively applicable remedies which have a wide action on all parts of the body. Constitutional remedies are polychrests.

Poly-herbal A term which is used to describe a nutritional supplement or medicinal product consisting of several species of herbs and other plant material. There is an increasing number of unlicensed poly-herbal products being marketed for quasi-medicinal purposes. Great care is needed to ensure proper selection of such products: the BAHNM can provide information about the legal status of individual products, and will advise on the use of herbs.

Pomegranate *(Punica granatum)* A shrub or small tree, native to Afghanistan and Pakistan, widely cultivated for its fruit. In medicine the rind is used against dysentry and the root bark as an anthelmintic.

POMs See **Prescription only medicines**.

Pompillion see **Burdock, greater**.

Pony Under modern terminology, a show pony must not exceed 14.2 hh although, in the early part of this century, the definition of a pony was 'a small horse less than 13 hh'. Polo 'ponies' are always referred to as ponies, whatever their actual height, while Arabian animals are always referred to as 'horses'.

Poppy There are two distinct species of poppy.
1. The opium poppy *(Papaver somniferum)*, also known as the white poppy. A sturdy annual plant reaching 1.5m in height, it prefers waste ground, but is also cultivated. Its natural habitat is south-eastern Europe and western Asia; it is not native to Britain, but is found occasionally as a relic of former culivation. The opium of which this poppy is the source was once described as 'the sheet anchor of the veterinarian'. The unripe seeds of the opium poppy are used in the manufacture of morphine and codeine, and tincture of opium produces laudanum. Externally, tincture and extract may be used to soothe pain; when used in conjunction with other medicines they are effective in joint and tendon injuries. Internally, they can have a purgative effect, and can be used

to control pain The plant is listed as a poison — see **Poisonous plants.** See also **Paracelsus**.

2. The field poppy *(Papaver rhoeas)* is also known as the red poppy, corn poppy and common poppy. An annual plant reaching around 70 cm in height,it has virtually world-wide distribution. It prefers waste places, often being found beside roads and railways. Although it is sometimes seen growing amongst arable crops, its presence has been dramatically reduced by pesticides. The field poppy contains toxic alkaloids and it is listed as a poisonous plant (see **Poisonous plants**) but it has an unpleasant taste and reports of poisoning are rare.

Posology   The study of the quantites of medicines to be administered.

Post mortem   Latin, meaning after death.

Posture   The Ancient Greeks defined the principles of classical riding technique some two thousand years ago. They understood how the rider could interfere with the horse's natural balance and co-ordination. Posture is the most important element of self- carriage, and good posture is central to good riding. The way that the horse is ridden is directly related to the potential for problems involving the musculo-skeletal system. See also **Alexander Technique**.

Potassium   A major mineral available in the horse's natural diet, quantities varying amongst individual foods. It is associated with fluid regulation, acid balance, nerve and muscle function and carbohydrate metabolism.

Potash   Potassium carbonate. A strong alkali originally obtained by preparing wood ash and evaporating it in pots, hence pot-ashes, potash. Formerly used widely in alternative remedies for the treatment of mange and grease, and also in antiseptic and diaphoretic remedies. Sometimes a constituent of horse balls.

Potato *(Solanum tuberosum)* The white underground tubers of the potatao are widely cultivated for human consumption, and have been used (cooked) as food for horses However, the stems, leaves, flowers and fruits (haulms) contain poisonous akaloids and the plant is listed as a poison — see **Poisonous plants.**

Potency The strength of a drug based on its ability to cause changes.

Potentilla erecta see **Tormentil**.

Poultice A hot preparation applied to the skin, often over a wound or other damage. Made by mixing up hot water and a medicinal compound.

Powder In medicine, a preparation of at least two drugs in the form of fine particles.

Practitioner This term used to be more closely associated with veterinary surgeons and doctors of human medicine, but it is now used more generally to include those practising other skills.

Precursor A substance from which another is formed.

Predisposition Susceptibility to a particular disease or condition; caused by direct or indirect genetic or environmental factors.

Pregnancy The period during which the mare is carrying the developing foetus.

Prescription only medicines Those which are legally restricted to use under the direction of a veterinary surgeon — for example, antibiotics. Compare **PMLs**.

Preservatives Substances used to prevent or delay decay.

Artificial preservatives are often found in feedstuffs; they are not compatible with the evolved physiology of the horse — see **Holistic feeding stuffs.and supplements**.

Privet *(Ligustrum spp.)* Common privet *(Ligustrum vulgare)* is a deciduous shrub native to Britain. Preferring calcareous soil, it can reach a height of 5m. Various types of privet, some of which are evergreen, are cultivated as garden shrubs or as ornamental hedging plants. Although its poisonous principle is not fully understood, the plant is poisonous and is listed as such – see **Poisonous plants**. Although the berries are the most toxic part, other parts have also caused poisoning.

Probiotics Live microbial feed additives, which can complement the natural gut bacteria that break down food. They can be useful in certain situations, but are not necessary on a regular basis if the horse is receiving proper nutrition. See **Holistic feeding stuffs and supplements**.

Product licence (Marketing authorisation) see **Medicines Acts**.

Prognosis A qualified medical opinion on the expected outcome of a disease or ailment.

Prolapse The downward displacement of a body part or tissue.

Prophylactic An act or procedure that prevents the development of a disease.

Proprietary name The name given to a product by its manufacturer, which may not be used by others: a trade name. Many drugs, which are of the same or similar composition as others, are marketed under different proprietary names. Compare **Generic name**.

Prosthesis Surgical insertion of foreign material to correct anatomical deficiency or injury.

Protein Complex substances made up from chains of building blocks called amino acids. Proteins are essential to the body, being associated with the maintenance of the structural material of muscles, tissues, organs etc. They are available from the horse's natural diet — see **Nutrition**.

Proud flesh Extraneous over-growth of tissue. Proud flesh often appears after injury to the legs, and can hinder the healing process. It is a rare phenomenon in natural medicine.

Proving The administration of a homoeopathic remedy to a healthy body sufficient to cause the symptoms noted in the *materia medica*.

Provitamin A substance which is not a vitamin in itself but which can be converted into a vitamin by the body.

Proximal Situated nearer to the centre of the body; thus the canon bone is proximal to the foot. Compare **Distal**.

Prunes Dried plums, traditionally used in laxative remedies.

Pruritis Itching, usually caused by local irritation but sometimes related to psychological factors.

Prussic acid Hydrocyanic acid: a solution of hydrogen and cyanide in water. A deadly poison which was formerly used in dilution as a sedative (for example, to reduce the spasms associated with tetanus) and to suppress skin irritations such as eczema.

Psora Hahnemann's term for the miasm of 'the itch' (scabies). Deficient reaction of the body to disease force. See reference to Hahnemann in **Homoeopathy**.

Psoriasis A chronic inflammation of the skin with scurf

formation. See **Mallenders and Sallenders**.

Psychology   The science of behaviour. Animal psychology is only just emerging as a formal discipline, consequently there are both qualified and unqualified practitioners. Unfortunately, proper veterinary research into animal psychology has progressed relatively slowly and, like other poorly understood disciplines, it is open to 'quackery'. Since there are no restrictions, anyone can set themselves up as an expert in this field: most are not members of the veterinary profession. See also **Cognitive ethology**.

Psyllium   The seeds of two species of plantain; one found in southern Europe, northern Africa and Asia, the other in India and Iran and also (cultivated) in Spain. Containing mainly mucilage and fixed oil, psyllium is traditionally used in medicine as a bulk laxative and demulcent.

Pteridium aquilinum   see **Bracken**.

'Puffing the glims'   As a horse gets older the hollows above the eyes become more pronounced. (deeper). 'Puffing the glims' is an old expression for the act of cutting a small hole in the skin near the hollow and blowing through a quill in order to fill the cavity with air, thus making the horse appear younger.

Pulmonary   Pertaining to the lungs.

Pulse   The rhythmic expansion of an artery in response to the pressure of the heart beat. The pulse of the horse may be felt at various points including at the lower jaw, in the hollow of the heel, inside the foreleg at knee level, and behind the elbow. The pulse should be regular and strong, and it should be about forty beats a minute in a healthy horse at rest, although this can vary.

Purgative   A remedy with drastic laxative action.

Pus A greenish or thick yellowish liquid which forms at the site of an infection. It consists of dead white blood cells, bacteria, partly destroyed tissue and protein.

Pyrethrum A former genus of composite plants now merged into the chrysanthemum family. Insecticidal powder was formerly made from various plants of the pyrethrum family. Synthetic equivalents (pyrethroids) of some of the active principles of pyrethrum flowers are commonly used in modern insecticides — see **Insecticide**.

Pyrexia Fever.

Pyridoxine Vitamin B6 -- see **Vitamins**.

Qi In oriental medicinal Qi (pronounced 'chee') is the body's energy, which must be balanced in order that good health can prevail. In illness the proper flow of Qi throughout the body is disturbed, and the physician uses various techniques, for example acupuncture, in order to re-balance it. See **Acupuncture**.

Quack An untrained and incompetent person, fraudulently claiming medical knowledge or skills, or attempting to sell fraudulent remedies. See **Medicines Acts**, **Farrier**, **Veterinary Surgeon**.

Quality Standard A pre-determined technical manufacturing standard against which the quality of products may be measured and assessed. See **Holistic feeding stuffs and supplements**.

Quarantine The method of preventing the spread of infectious disease by isolating infected individuals.

Quassia The bitter extract of the wood and dark bark of a West Indian tree, *Picrasma excelsa*. A traditional remedy for digestive problems.

Quicksilver see **Mercury**.

Quidding The term used to describe a quantity of food being rejected from the mouth. This happens either immediately after the food is taken, or after partial mastication. It is usually associated with a problem involving the horse's teeth.

Quinine A drug originally derived from cinchona and used for the prevention and treatment of malaria in humans. See **Homoeopathy, Cinchona, Sulphate of Quinine**.

Quittor Persistent suppurating sinus of the foot which has its opening at or near the coronet. The cause is an infection of the lateral cartilage from which the resultant pus takes the line of least resistance to the surface of the skin.

Radionics A form of instrumented medical radiaesthesia, which was developed by the distinguished American physician Dr Albert Abrams in the 1920s. Further developments were made in the 1930s by Ruth Drown, an American chiropractor. Radionics instrumentation has become more sophisticated over the years and today it is a valuable aid to the early detection of potentially serious disease. It is increasingly used for horses, being affectionately known as the 'black box'. Unfortunately, because of the nature of radionics, it lends itself to malpractice and exploitation by unqualified and unskilled practitioners. See also **Medical radiaesthesia**.

Ragwort *(Senecio jacobaea)* A (usually) biennial plant, abundant in Britain, reaching 30—100cm high, preferring waste land, roadsides and pastures. It has bright yellow flowers on erect stems and jagged, lobed leaves, hence its name. The plant contains toxic alkaloids and is listed as a poison (see **Poisonous plants**). Although some species, notably deer and rabbits, seem resistant to ragwort poisoning, cattle and horses are especially susceptible. Horses rarely take the plant while it is growing, but will readily consume it in wilted form, when broken off in the field, or incorporated into hay. Ragwort is a common cause of serious or fatal poisoning in horses and it was designated an injurious weed in the *Weeds Act 1959*. Under this legislation, land-owners can be required to prevent certain plants from spreading, and failure to do so within a specified time renders them liable to prosecution.

Rain scald see **Mud fever**.

Raking An old term for the practice of introducing the hand into the rectum and drawing out any hardened faeces which the horse may have difficulty in voiding.

Rape A plant of the Brassica family cultivated for its herbage and oil-producing seeds. The name is applied to several sim-ilar species. Rape oil was formerly used as an ingredient in horse balls to give them consistency and mass. Crops are a common cause of respiratory problems for horses living or exercising in the area. 'Headshaking' has also been blamed on this crop.

Rash An inflammation of the skin, usually involving itching and reddening. A rash may be either a local skin reaction or a symptom of other bodily disorders.

Rasping Removal of sharp edges from the teeth using a rasp or file. Horses' teeth are open rooted and continue grow throughout life to compensate for the wear and tear caused by the constant grinding of food. Occasionally teeth escape wear and develop uneven sharp edges which, if left, may cause eating difficulties. A veterinary surgeon should be consulted if a horse shows difficulty in chewing or 'quids' its food (see **Quidding**). Equine dentists, if properly qualified, are also competent to carry out such work.

Recapitulation The recurrence of past elements of a chronic disease (often seemingly unrelated to present symptoms) as a result of homoeopathic treatment. These past elements are usually symptoms suppressed by antiopathy.

Red fescue *(Festuca rubra)* A species of grass recommended for horse pastures. See **Meadow**.

Reflex An automatic or involuntary bodily response to a stimulus.

Regulatory remedy In homoeopathy, a remedy which has opposite action at high and low potencies.

Rehydration Replacement of fluids lost in dehydration.

Relapse The reappearance of the symptoms of a disease after a period of apparent improvement.

Relaxant The name given to a substance which relaxes nerves and muscles.

Remedial farriery The practice of shoeing horses in a particular way to take account of certain physical characterics or medical conditions. These may be associated with abnormalities of the hoof, conformation and movement, etc., and also with disease. With some diseases, proper remedial farriery is essential if the horse is to continue being ridden, and this is best carried out under the direction of the veterinary surgeon attending. See also **Shoes**.

Remedy A means of curing a disease.

Renal Relating to or affecting the kidneys.

Repertory A dictionary of symptoms, with indicated remedies.

Resins In medicine, hard, brittle secretions from various plants, such as hops and myrrh, which soften on heating.

Respiration The vital process of gaseous exchange whereby oxygen is taken into the body and carbon dioxide is expelled.

Respiratory system The organs and tissues involved in the process of respiration. The system includes all the airways involved in the process of transporting air to and from the lungs.

Restorative The name given (especially in herbal medicine) to a substance which restores normal physiological activity.

Retinol Vitamin A – see **Vitamins**.

Rhamnus cathartica see **Buckthorn**.

Rheumatism A common term for any aches and pains affecting the joints or muscles.

Rheum rhaponticum see **Rhubarb**.

Rhinovirus, adenovirus In common with equine influenza and equine herpes virus, these two viruses are associated with a runny nose and elevated temperature. Treatment consists of minimising the potential for secondary infections, and ensuring that the horse has clean air.

Rhododendron *(Rhododendron ponticum)* An evergreen shrub up to 3m high, common in Britain, being found in woodland and cultivated in gardens and parks. The leaves, pollen, flowers and nectar of many species contain toxic substances, but it does not usually present a risk to horses unless they gain access to land, or garden rubbish, containing it.

In 400 BC Xenophon reported the poisoning of Greek soldiers by honey made naturally from wild rhododendrons. In Britain, poisoning by honey is virtually unknown; little nectar is taken by bees from rhododendron flowers, and honey made in the spring (when the rhododendron is in bloom) is left in the hives for the bees themselves.

Rhubarb *(Rheum rhaponticum)* A large perennial plant commonly cultivated in gardens for human consumption. Rhubarb has been used for generations as a laxative and purgative for horses. However, the leaves contain an irritant poison and the plant should not be used except under expert guidance.

Riboflavin Also known as lactoflavin. Vitamin B2 – see **Vitamins**.

Ricinus communis see **Castor oil**.

Rig A male horse in whom one or both testes do not descend into the scrotal sac at the usual time of sexual development. The term also describes a horse who has been inadequately castrated, and who consequently exhibits some of the characteristics of a stallion.

Rigor An attack of shivering accompanied by a rapid rise in body temperature, which often marks the onset of a fever.

Rigor mortis The stiffening of a body caused by chemical changes occurring within muscle tissue several hours after death. It starts to disappear after about 24 hours.

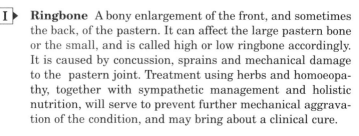

Ringbone A bony enlargement of the front, and sometimes the back, of the pastern. It can affect the large pastern bone or the small, and is called high or low ringbone accordingly. It is caused by concussion, sprains and mechanical damage to the pastern joint. Treatment using herbs and homoeopathy, together with sympathetic management and holistic nutrition, will serve to prevent further mechanical aggravation of the condition, and may bring about a clinical cure.

Ringworm A skin disorder caused by any of a group of several fungi which spread from horse to horse, sometimes through contaminated tack. The condition is recognisable by groups of scabby areas appearing in raised rings on the skin, hence the name. Treatment is through inhibition of the organism by topical application of medicine, and by stimulation of the horse's immune system using holistic nutrition and therapy. General cleanliness is important in controlling the spread.

Roaring and whistling Abnormal sounds on inhalation made by vibrations of the slackened vocal cords on one or both sides of the larynx. Roaring and whistling differ only in the pitch of sound: in roaring the pitch is low, and in whistling it is high. The condition is a consequence of paralysis in associated muscles, which may arise from hereditary factors or disease.

Rock salt A solid mass of salt which the horse may ingest by licking as required.

Rosehips *(Rosa rugosa, R. canina)* The fruit of the rose. Rosehips are a source of natural biotin, vitamin C, and other nutrients which promote, among other things, healthy hoof growth. In common with all nutrients which are provided as part of the whole plant, nutrients in this form are far superior to any purified source.

Rosin Also known as colophony. A resin obtained from pine wood. Formerly used as a diuretic.

Roughage Low energy, high fibre materials such as hay and other herbage, which the horse has evolved to eat. The greater part of the diet must be provided in this form, otherwise digestive problems can occur.

Rough-stalked meadow grass *(Poa trivialis)* A species of grass recommended for horse pasture. See **Meadow.**

Rowelling see **Blistering**.

Rubefacient The name given to a substance that produces a gentle reddening and warming of the skin.

Rubus fruticosis See **Blackberry**.

Rupture The splitting open or apart of a tissue or organ.

Rutaceae cusparia see **Angostura**.

Ryegrass *(Lolium perenne)* A species of grass recommended for horse pastures. See **Meadow**.

Saddling The horse's way of going is directly related to saddlery and tack. Correct saddle fitting is central to the horse's comfort and welfare. The potential for physical problems developing will be greatly reduced by regular attention to this crucial and often neglected requirement. See **Holistic saddles and registered holistic saddle fitters**.

Sago A nutritious, mealy substance obtained from the pith of the Metroxylon palm and other similar species. Traditionally used to make a mash which was given to sick horses who were off their feed.

Sainfoin *(Onobrychis viciafolia)* A nutritious leguminous fodder plant, related to lucerne. Traditionally, sainfoin hay is highly regarded for horses.

Sal ammoniac Ammonium chloride, traditionally mixed with vinegar and water to make an embrocation for strains and bruises.

Saliva A clear alkaline fluid secreted by the salivary glands and mucous membrane of the mouth. Consisting chiefly of water, mucus and enzymes, its functions are to lubricate the inside of the mouth, to moisten food during mastication, and to begin the chemical process of digestion.

Salix alba see **Willow**.

Sallenders see **Mallenders**.

Salt Sodium chloride, existing naturally as a mineral and in solution in seawater, brine-springs etc. Salt is required by the body, and is usually added to compound feeds. The performance horse requires extra salt to compensate for its loss through sweating, and a salt lick should always be available. However, care should be taken not to over-supplement salt.

Salt was traditionally used as a purgative, and as an appetite restorer for sick horses. It was also used to expel worms, and was applied to malignant ulcers and sores in an attempt to destroy the seat of infection. As it was commonly used on urban roads during winter-time to dispel snow and ice, it often engendered problems such as cracked heels in horses who were constantly exposed to it.

Saltpetre Potassium nitrate. Traditionally used as a febrifuge, diuretic and alterative, being very popular in alterative remedies for reducing filled legs.

Sal volatile Also known as smelling salts. Ammonium carbonate, or a solution of it in alcohol and/or ammonia in water. Traditionally used to quicken the pulse and respiration rate, particularly after operations under chloroform.

Salycilic acid A chemical compound present in plants such as meadowsweet and willow and the basis of the proprietary drug, aspirin. The word aspirin is derived from *Spirea ulmaria*, the Latin name for the meadoweet plant from which salycilic acid was originally isolated.

Sambucus nigra see **Elder**.

Sand cracks Cracks in the hoof wall which either begin at the top of the hoof and extend downwards, or at the bottom and extend upwards. They vary in severity; many horses who develop sand cracks never go lame, but others have to be turned away and receive medical attention. There are certain areas of the hoof which are especially likely to be affected, such as the inner quarters of the front feet. The strength of the horn fibres, which is closely associated with nutrition, is an important consideration in preventing the condition. Shavings in stable bedding may contribute to the condition.

Sanguisorba officianalis see **Burnet, greater**.

Sanitas A traditional proprietary antiseptic fluid, containing eucalyptus and pine oil.

Santonin An anthelmintic extracted from a species of wormwood, see **Wormwood.**

Saponins Found in plant material, saponins form a lather (*sapo* means soap) when they are mixed with water. They also emulsify oils. Some saponins are diuretic, others are expectorant; most are highly toxic.

Sarcoid A fleshy tumour.

Sarothamnus scoparius see **Broom**.

Sassafras (*Sassafras officinale*) A North American tree; a member of the laurel family. The bark and roots yield a powerful stimulant traditionally used in the treatment of digestive problems.

Savine (*Juniperus sabina*) A species of juniper which produces a toxic irritant volatile oil which is anthelmintic and abortifacient. The name is also extended to other species. Savine was traditionally used with opium in lotions for infected sores etc., and mixed with lard or wax to keep open setons or rowels — see **Setons, Rowelling**.

Scab A hard crust of dried matter, consisting of dried blood, serum, or pus, that develops over a wound.

Scalpel A small surgical knife with a pointed end. Modern scalpels have detachable, single-use blades.

Scouring Diarrhoea.

Scrotum The flexible fleshy sac that holds the testes outside the abdominal cavity. Efficient production and storage of spermatozoa are dependent upon a temperature somewhat lower than that of the abdomen. The scrotum maintains the optimum temperature of the testes by contracting and expanding, thus moving them nearer or further away from the heat of the body as required.

Seaweed see **Bladderwrack**, **Kelp**.

Sebum An oily liquid secreted onto the surface of the skin by the subaceous glands. Sebum prevents excessive dryness of hair and skin; it is also mildly anti-bacterial. See **Grease**.

Secretion The release of chemical substances from glands. Compare **Excretion**.

Sedative A substance that reduces nervousness and anxiety and induces sleep.

Seedy toe Separation of the horn of the hoof, which may occur at any part between the toe and the heel. It is associated with inflammation of the coronet.

Selenium A trace element available in the horse's natural diet, quantities varying amongst individual foods. Associated with the maintenance of normal muscle tissue.

Semen The sperm-containing fluid which is ejaculated from the penis at the climax of mating.

Semi-wilted forage Grass that has been cut and compressed into plastic bags, which are then heat sealed. The mild fermentation which goes on inside the bag prevents damaging fungal spores from developing. Nevertheless, these products do not suit all horses; a significant amount of diarrhoea has been observed in some horses fed on them. See also **Silage**.

Senna A kind of cinnamon shrub which yields a purgative from its leaves. Senna has been valued in both human and veterinary medicine for many centuries. In ancient Egypt it was so highly prized that it was reserved for the aristocracy and known as the 'guardian of the royal bowel movement'. Senna as traditionally used as a laxative in equine medicine, sometimes together with sodium sulphate (glaubers salt) — see **Glaubers salt**.

Sepsis The destruction of tissues by disease-causing bacteria. Sepsis can either be a simple local problem, or more general in nature, causing serious illness.

Septic Pertaining to sepsis.

Septicaemia The presence of large numbers of disease-producing organisms circulating in the blood. Symptoms include high fever, shivering and rapid breathing, possibly leading to coma and death. Compare **Toxaemia**.

Serum The clear fluid that separates from blood which has been allowed to stand.

Sesamoiditis The sesamoid bones lie behind the fetlock. When the ligaments holding them are over-strained, sesamoiditis develops. The severity of the condition depends upon the degree of strain — in some instances the ligaments are torn, and will take a long time to heal. Fracture of one or both of the sesamoid bones themselves sometimes occurs, which is obviously more serious. Holistic treatment revolves around judicious exercise, laser therapy, and natural medcines including herbal and homoeopathic remedies.

Setfast see **Azoturia**.

Setons Pieces of tape or cord placed either through or at the base of abscesses or ulcers with deep sinuses, or set to run beneath the skin. This obsolete practice was intended to speed the healing of troublesome infections by enabling the removal of pus from the core of the wound. The seton was inserted by means of a sharp instrument, such as a needle, leaving long ends which were knotted to hold the seton in place, and then tied together. The knots were released and the seton was pulled backwards and forwards, then cleaned and replaced regularly, the object being to keep the wound open and draining. See **Savine**, **Rowelling**.

Shiatsu Acupressure massage, see **Acupressure**.

Shoes Artificial wearing surfaces, usually fashioned from steel and nailed to the underside edge of the horse's hooves. Normal shoes are open at the heel, forming a roughly 'U' shape. Correct fitting of shoes is essential to the horse's well-being, and the skill of the farrier is paramount in ensuring that shoes are well-fitted and comfortable.

The condition of the horse's shoes should be constantly checked. Any problems which arise from faulty shoeing are obviously increased by the weight of the rider. Such problems may not be confined to the horse's feet – there is often a knock-on effect. For example, a badly placed nail may cause pain which could cause the horse to change his way of going, and this may place abnormal strain on other parts of his body. In the same way, incorrectly 'balanced' feet will cause problems elsewhere (joint strain, etc.). See also **Remedial farriery**.

Shock Clinical shock may be caused by severe mental or physical trauma; it can occur after haemorrhage, surgery, burns and scalds, sudden decrease in the heart's pumping action etc. Symptoms include: weakness; pale and cold mucous membranes and extremities; sub-normal temperature, but no shivering; a weak and rapid pulse; shallow, quickened breathing.

Sialagogue A substance which produces an increased flow of saliva.

Sidebone Ossification of the lateral cartilages of the foot. In young horses it is regarded as an unsoundness, but it is not regarded as being so serious in older animals, since most eventually develop cartilage ossification to some degree. It is a condition associated with hard work and used to be common in draught horses, although any type of animal may develop the problem.

Side-effect An unwanted physical or mental effect produced by the use of a medicine. Side- effects are normally associated with modern technological drugs and are hardly, if ever, caused by properly used holistic medicines.

Side line A restraint to prevent kicking. It is made from a length of rope or leather placed around the horse's neck and fastened like a collar, having loose ends which are fastened around one (single side line), or both (double side line) of the hind heels. The double side line is also employed to cast the horse when required — see **Cast**.

Side rod A stiff rod fastened at one end to the horse's head-collar and at the other end to the girth. Fitted to restrict the backward and downward movement of the horse's head, thus preventing chewing of dressings, etc. See also **Cradle**.

Sign Any observable evidence of the presence of disease. See also **Symptom**.

Silage fodder such as grass, preserved by 'pickling' it in its own juice. Feeding silage to horses is not without risk, as it may contain potentially lethal micro-organisms if not prepared correctly. Good quality silage can be a substitute for hay, but the risks involved in feeding it makes it unpopular. See also **Semi-wilted forage**.

Silk see **Suture**.

Similimum In homoeopathy, a remedy closely matching the symptoms exhibited by the patient: the ideal homoeopathic remedy.

Sinew A tendon.

Singeing The practice of removing long hairs using a flame after the horse has been clipped. Singeing lamps powered by gas were formerly used for this purpose, which has generally been rendered obsolete by the development of efficient electric clippers.

Sinus 1) Any of the air cavities within the bones of the skull.
2) An infected tract leading from the point of infection to the surface of the skin or to a hollow organ.

Skeleton The rigid framework of bones which gives the body form and protects and supports the organs and tissues. It also provides anchorage for muscles and forms a system of levers essential for locomotion.

Skin The waterproof, elastic outer covering of the body which protects it from injury and invasion by hostile organisms. It also plays an important role in maintaining correct body temperature, through the cooling effect of evaporating sweat during and after exercise.

Sleep A state of natural unconsciousness, during which there is no sign of brain activity apart from the maintenance of basic bodily functions.

Slippery elm *(Ulmus fulva)* The inner bark of a small tree of eastern and central North America. Used internally in herbal medicine as a lubricant and for the relief of gastro-intestinal irritation, it is one of the best soothing remedies and is good for diarrhoea. Externally, it is useful in poultices as a healing agent for wounds.

Slough Dead tissue which separates from healthy tissue and falls away.

Small airway disease Also known as 'broken wind', 'heaves' or COPD (chronic obstructive pulmonary disease). Airborne moulds in stable dust are thought to be the root cause, although the condition is often associated with sensitisation through reaction to viral diseases, or possibly to vaccination. As with the treatment of other diseases of the respiratory tract, clean air is essential. Holistic management of the disease involves helping the body's own defences through holistic nutrition and medicines.

Smegma thick, cheesy, foul-smelling secretion in the sheath of the penis.

Smelling salts see **Sal volatile**.

Smooth-stalked meadow grass *(Poa pratensis)* A species of grass – see **Meadow**.

Smutts, Jan Christian (1870-1950) A South African philosopher and scientist, Smutts was the first person to define the principles and theory of holism in modern scientific language. See **Holism**, **Holistic feeding stuffs and supplements**.

Snakeroot *(Persicaria bisorta)* A hairless perennial with twisted roots, hence its traditional name. Otherwise known as bistort. Found in western and central Europe, northern Asia and North America, snakeroot prefers open woodland, damp meadows and roadsides. Traditionally used as an antiseptic wash for external wounds, also internally for the treatment of diarrhoea. It promotes reflex expectoration and salivation, and also acts as a peripheral circulatory stimulant and diaphoretic.

Soap Traditional soft soap was formerly used in various remedies and was often included as an ingredient in horse balls. Soap has a purgative affect, but its use was limited in that it reduced the effect of stronger purgatives such as aloes. Externally, when mixed with turpentine and alcohol, it was used in embrocations for the treatment of strains and bruises.

Socket In anatomy, a hollow depression into which another part fits, as in a ball and socket joint.

Sodium A major mineral available in the horse's natural diet, quantities varying amongst individual foods.It is associated with regulating the body fluid, with the transmission of nerve impulses, and the absorption of sugars and amino acids.

Sodium Sulphate see **Glaubers salt**.

Soil analysis The chemical profile of the soil will determine which species of grasses and herbage will thrive in it. Soil analysis carried out by a laboratory is an integral part of good pasture management for horses — see **Meadow**. Soil analysis and advice on pasture management is available through the BAHNM.

Soil Association see **Organic**.

Solanum dulcamara see **Bittersweet**.

Solanum nigrum see **Black nightshade.**

Solution Usually a liquid, consisting of two or more dissimilar substances, in which a solid is dissolved.

Solution of acetate of ammonium A chemical preparaton formerly mixed with spirit of nitric ether and used to promote sweating in cases of infectious fever, bronchitis, etc.

Solution of ammonia (strong) A chemical preparation formerly used as a counter-irritant — see **Firing**. Also mixed with turpentine and applied as a dressing for sprains to tendons and ligaments. Used internally in cases of flatulence and applied topically for the treatment of some insect stings.

Solution of chromic acid A chemical preparation which was formerly used as a disinfectant, deodorizer and caustic. Popular in the treatment of ulcerating wounds and also used in solution as an application to 'greasy legs'. When mixed with tar, it was used as a dressing for thrush and canker of the foot.

Solvent A fluid in which a substance is dissolved. In homoeopathy it is usually an alcohol and water mixture.

Sore A septic wound of the skin or mucous membrane.

Soundness A horse is said to be sound when he is free from hereditary disease, is in possession of natural health and is of good constitution. Unusual or undesirable conformation is not of itself unsoundness, but it may lead to unsoundness in some circumstances.

Southernwood (*Artemisia arbrotanum*) A shrubby plant indigenous to Spain and Italy but widely cultivated elsewhere. An aromatic bitter herb traditionally used in fomentations, as a digestive tonic, an anthelmintic and a uterine stimulant. As is the case with many herbs, it should not be used during pregnancy.

Soya *(Glycine max* or *Glycine soja)* An eastern Asiatic papillionaceous plant. Soya bean meal has a protein content of up to 50%. It can be used as the sole source of supplementary protein in the horse's diet.

Spanish fly see **Cantharides**.

Spasm A brief or sustained involuntary muscular contraction. Spasms may result from muscle disorders, diseases of the nervous system, or habit.

Spavin Spavin occurs in two forms.
  Bone spavin is arthritis of the hock joint. It involves the lower bones of the joint and, like all arthritic conditions, it may have many predisposing factors, such as conformation. Injuries such as strain on the hock joint, particularly during fast exercise, may also be associated with the condition.
  Bog spavin produces a soft, chronic and fluctuating enlargement of the joint capsule of the hock. It appears on the inner and upper part of the joint. The condition is particularly associated with strain and it is aetiologically similar to bone spavin.
  Holistic nutrition and correct saddling, together with the healing stimulus of natural medicines, are usually effective in restoring proper function of the joint and preventing fusion of the small bones.

Species A group of individuals having common characteristics and being able to inter-breed and produce fertile offspring. Similar species are grouped together as a 'genus'.

Speedwell *(Veronica officinalis)* A perennial plant preferring heaths, dry grassland, open woodland and poor pasture. Traditionally used as a digestive tonic and in the treatment of diarrhoea.

Sperm The mature male sex cell (spermatozoon) which posesses a tail, enabling it to reach and fertilise the ovum after introduction into the female's reproductive tract.

Sphincter A strong ring of muscle which, when contracted, closes off a passage-way within the body. An example is the anal sphincter, around the anus.

Spirit of nitrous ether A chemical preparation formerly used as a stimulant, anti-spasmodic and diuretic. Given in cases of chills, fevers and colic.

Spirit of salt A mixture of sulphuric acid, common salt and water, formerly used as a caustic in the treatment of foul ulcers and other deep-seated infections. Also once popular for the treatment of canker and wounds of the foot.

Splint A hard, bony swelling which appears under the skin, normally on the forelegs, but occasionally on the hind. Splints are associated with the splint bone, hence the name. As with many bony problems associated with the legs, concussion can play a part in their development. Conformation and lack of balance — especially that causing uneven weight distribution — are also implicated. Splints can vary in size from something like a pea up to a hen's egg. Treatment depends upon the severity of the problem; some splints will resolve and almost disappear without treatment at all. New splints rarely occur in horses above seven years of age.

Spore Small reproductive forms produced by plants and other organisms.

Sprain An injury to a ligament or tendon caused by over-stretching. Injuries of this sort occur most commonly in horses used for competition, damage being most frequently seen in the flexor tendons of the front limbs. Compare **Strain**.

Sputum A mixture of saliva and mucus coughed up from the respiratory tract. In the case of disease, the consistency and colour of the mucus can aid diagnosis.

Squill *(Urginea maritima)* Also known as the sea squill, this hairless perennial plant is found by the sea on the Mediterranean coastline. Other types *(Scilla autumnalis* and *s verna)* grow in coastal pastures of the British Isles. The plants are traditionally used to provide expectorants, laxatives and diuretics. However, certain species are toxic, and squills should be used only by experienced practitioners.

Stable vices Vices which are a nuisance in the stable — see also **Vices**.

Staling The term given to equine urination.

Starch The principle reserve food material stored in plants; chemically, a carbohydrate. Traditionally used (often mixed with chalk) to modify the effect of pungent medicines. See also **Carbohydrate**.

Statutory Statement A compulsory statement of certain information to be made on the packaging of feedstuffs as required by the *Feeding Stuffs Regulations 1991*. The Statutory Statement must be displayed on every product. It must include specified information, set out and expressed in the required form, which must be clearly separated from any other information carried on the product.

While the Statutory Statement will give an indication as to the raw materials used, the true nature of some of them may not be obvious because 'generic terms' can be used. For example 'oils and fats' may be either animal or vegetable fats; 'wheatfeed' is a by-product of the milling industry.

There is also provision for a voluntary declaration of additional information, but this is rarely given.

Stellaria media see **Chickweed.**

Sterile 1) Unable to reproduce.
2) Entirely free from organisms capable of causing infection.

Steroid Sterol-related substances having a chemical configuration based on an unsaturated hydrocarbon, cyclopetenophenanthrene. Synthetic analogues also exist, which counteract the effects of homoeopathy and other natural medicines. See also **Corticosteroid**.

Stimulant A substance that promotes increased activity of bodily system or function.

⟩ **St John's Wort** *(Hypericum perforatum)* An erect, hairless plant growing to about 1m.in height, preferring rocky slopes, dry grassland, meadows and open woods. Common in many parts of the world and most of Britain, although rare in parts of Scotland. Used medicinally for healing wounds, for sprains and bruises, and for rheumatism; also used internally for intestinal problems. The plant causes a condition known as photosensitisation in which the skin becomes sensitive to sunlight and develops small lesions on its surface. It is a listed poison.

Stockholm tar Also known as fir-tar. A traditional emollient ointment.

Stomachic An agent that promotes the secretory activity of the stomach; an appetite stimulant and tonic.

Stopping The practice of applying substances to the horse's feet in order to try and prevent them from drying out and becoming brittle. Traditionally, horses who worked on hard roads were considered to need stopping on a regular basis and a mixture of cow-dung and clay was often used for this purpose. Felt pads wetted with water and fastened on the feet overnight was another method.

Straights Individual feedstuffs such as oats, barley, etc., as opposed to commercially formulated rations.

Strain 1) Exessive working of muscles so as to cause the fibres to overstretch or tear, resulting in pain and swelling. Strains are common in competition horses; proper fitness is essential to keep them to a minimum. Compare **Sprains**.

2) A group of individuals having certain properties which distinguish them from others of the same species.

Strangulation Closure or constriction of a passageway within the body, for example, within the gut.

Straw The stalks of cereal plants such as wheat or barley after the grain has been removed. Horses with good teeth may be given small quantities of straw since it is a good source of fibre. However, it should be given only in small quantities as it has comparatively little energy value.

Stress Any physical or psychological factor which may threaten the health and well-being of the body, or have an adverse effect on its functioning. Constant psychological stress brings about chemical changes in the body and may predispose the horse to many ailments; certain individuals being more prone to it than others. See also **Behavioural problems**.

Striking Describes the injury of a forelimb by a hind limb. It can sometimes result from pelvic misalignment.

Stringhalt A condition which usually affects the hind limbs. The foot is brought upwards toward the body in a jerky movement and is held there for a moment, before being forced hard down to the floor again. Stringhalt is thought to be associated with a malfunction of the nervous system; the muscle spasms which typify the condition can be brought on by certain movements, such as turning sharply; but they can also occur during slow movement. Holistic medicines and nutrition and chiropractic manipulation of the spine have been known to help.

Strophanthus *(Strophanthus hispidus)* An African and Asiatic genus of the periwinkle family, the extracts of which are used as arrow poison by local hunters. In medicine it can be used as an alternative to digitalis; it is more readily absorbed and the effects on the body are not so enduring. Because of its toxicity it should be used only by suitably experienced veterinarians.

Strychnine see **Nux vomica**.

Stupor A state of reduced consciousness, short of coma, in which there is apparent lack of mental activity and reduced response to stimuli. Compare **Coma**.

Styptic A substance that stops bleeding.

Styrax A genus of plants, *Styracaceae*, rich in resinous and aromatic substances. Traditionally used in the treatment of lung disorders and fevers.

Sub-clinical Describes a disease which has not yet manifested itself sufficiently for clinical observation.

Subcutaneous Beneath the skin. See **Injection**.

Sublimed sulphur A chemical preparation used in alterative remedies. Also mixed with linseed oil and oil of tar, or formed into an ointment with lard, to destroy skin parasites.

Succussion In homoeopathy, the process of violent shaking of a solution of a substance. It is part of the preparation of the remedies, transforming them into higher potencies. During succussion the molecular structure of the solution is magnetically changed. See **Homoeopathy**.

Sucrose A carbohydrate. Sucrose is a major constituent of sugar beet and cane sugar.

Sudorific see **Diaphoretics**.

Sugar A sweet substance obtained chiefly from sugar beet and sugar cane. The name is also extended to any member of the same class of carbohydrates. Molasses and sugars under different names are often included in horse feeds. However, in this form, divorced from their co-constituents, they are not compatible with the evolved physiological requirements of the horse. See **Holistic feeding stuffs and supplements**, **Behavioural problems**.

Sugar beet Normally supplied as dried pellets or shreds, often with molasses added to make it more palatable, sugar beet is a by-product of sugar manufacture. In its dry state it can cause choking and will swell in the stomach, so it must be thoroughly soaked before use. It is commonly fed to many types of horses, providing instant energy in the form of sugar (from the molasses) and slow-release energy from the fibrous content. Products containing non-constituent sugars such as molasses are not recommended by holistic veterinarians, as they may be linked to digestive and behavioural problems, and affect the immune system. Molasses-free sugar beet is therefore to be preferred. See **Holistic feeding stuffs and supplements**, **Sugar**.

Sulphate of copper A chemical preparation also known as blue vitriol or bluestone, formerly used as a mild caustic and astringent. Applied externally to promote the healing of wounds and to check the formation of proud flesh; used internally as a tonic and astringent.

Sulphate of iron A chemical prepartion formerly used as a tonic, astringent and styptic. It was given in debilitating and wasting diseases, and to arrest mucous discharge in nasal catarrh. Also used to suppress bleeding in cases of capilliary haemorrhage.

Sulphate of quinine A chemical preparation formerly used as a tonic in cases of general debility, or following disease. Also given during fevers as an anti-pyretic.

Sulphate of zinc A chemical preparation formerly used as an external treatment for wounds. It was. applied in order to speed the healing process and to prevent the growth of proud flesh.

Sulpherated antimony A chemical preparation formerly used as an alterative.

Sulphurated potash A chemical preparation formerly used in the treatment of some chronic skin conditions, and as an anti-parasitic.

Sulphur A non-metallic element used in preparations for skin disorders and infections. Sulphur is active against fungus and parasites and is present in plants such as the marigold see **Marigold**.

Sulphuric acid A powerful chemical formerly used as a caustic for the removal of warts and proud flesh. In dilute form, it was traditionally given as an antidote to lead-poisoning, and it was used as a tonic in combination with vegetable bitters.

Sulphurous acid A chemical preparation formerly used in conjunction with glycerine in the treatment of ringworm. Also used in gaseous form to disinfect stables.

Superficial In anatomy, situated near the surface, hence the superficial blood vessels are those close to the surface of the skin.

Superior In anatomy, referring to an organ or part which is situated higher than another point of reference in the body. Compare **Inferior**.

Supplements see **Nutritional supplements**.

Suppository A suspension of medicine in a soft base, such as cocoa butter, which may be inserted for absorption via the rectum or anus.

Suppuration The formation and discharge of pus.

Surfactant A wetting agent which acts by reducing surface tension.

Surfeit An old term for eruptions of skin, similar to nettle rash. See **Urticaria**.

Suture 1)In surgery, a material used to sew tissue together to facilitate healing. Usually made from silk, catgut, nylon or wire. The use of silk and catgut (made from sheep's intestine) has declined, largely because of the development of sythetic sutures. Other materials, such as horse-hair and thread, were formerly used.

2)Describes the joints between the bones of the skull.

Swab A pad of absorbent material such as loose- woven cotton gauze, used to clean out or apply medication to wounds, or to clean out body cavities.

Sweat A watery fluid containing body chemicals, principally electrolytes (salts), secreted by the sweat glands of the skin. Sweating is a means by which the body temperature is regulated through the cooling effects of evaporation. The horse sweats profusely during and after hard exercise, therefore precautions should be taken to prevent dehydration and chilling after hard work.

Swedes Swedish turnips. Traditionally fed as an admixture to the horse's food in order to provide variety. They should be fed cooked.

Sweet flagroot The roots of the hairless perennial plant, *Acorus calamus*, found growing in wet habitats in Europe, Asia and North America. Traditionally used as a digestive stimulant.

Sweet itch One of the most common manifestations of skin allergies. It is mostly seen in pony and cob breeds. The allergy is associated with the bites of a midge, which is particularly prevalent during the summer months, especially June and July. Sunlight and grass proteins may play a part in the aetiology. Commonly affected areas are the shoulders, withers, mane, loins and quarters, especially around the base of the tail. The condition is very irritating to the horse and the affected part may become raw and inflamed, as a result of constant rubbing on convenient objects such as trees in an attempt to relieve the itching. The areas affected often lose hair, and the skin may ooze serum. Treatment consists of reducing exposure to the midges (where this is practical), together with dietary adjustments aimed at reducing future susceptibility. Non-synthetic fly sprays, which will repel the midges, are available, and garlic and other herbs may be given to make the coat less attractive to them. The affected skin may be treated with topical application of aromatic essential oils to deter midges, and healing creams or lotions may be applied. Homoeopathy is usually effective.

Sycosis A Hahnemannian term which describes excessive body reaction to a disease force. See reference to Hahnemann in **Homoeopathy**.

Symbiosis A close obligatory association of two organisms which act together for the benefit of both.

Symphytum officinale see **Comfrey**.

Symptom A detected abnormality which is used in the diagnosis of disease.

Syndrome Collection of signs and symptoms usually classed as a disease entity and given a name.

Synergy The interaction of substances which, when given together, produce a different or greater effect than when the substances are given separately. Successful use of herbal medicine, homoeopathy and remedial nutrition rely on a detailed knowledge of this principle.

Synovial fluid The thick, clear liquid which lubricates joints and tendons. It is secreted by the synovial membrane.

Synthesised Manufactured or artificially produced. Compare **Natural**.

Syringe An instrument, consisting of a piston contained in a tubular body and connected to a needle or tube. Used to give injections or to remove material from part of the body.

Syrup see **Molasses**.

Syrup of buckthorn A traditional purgative administered in horse balls, cotaining buckthorn, ginger, pimento and sugar, these ingredients being placed in a cloth and boiled in water until a syrup is formed.

Tablet In pharmacy, a small disc of compressed powders containing one or more drugs for oral administration.

Tabanidae see **Gadfly**.

Tallow Rendered fat, especially of cows or sheep.

Tamarind *(Tamarindus indica)* A large tropical tree bearing a fruit containing a sweet, dark-reddish pulp, which was often a constituent of traditional electuaries — see **Electuary**.

Tamus communis see **Bryony, black**.

Tannic acid An astringent derived from oak bark and used in tanning leather; also traditionally used in the treatment of bowel disorders, to check secretion, and as an antidote to poisons. See **Oak bark**, **Tannins**, **Tannic acid jelly**.

Tannic acid jelly A traditional ointment containing tannic acid, used in the treatment of burns. See **Oak bark**, **Tannic acid**, **Tannins**.

Tannins Substances which have a mainly astringent action on the body. They have the effect of shrinking cells by pre-cipitating proteins from their surface. Astringents may be used internally or externally, and are often used in lotions to protect and harden the skin. They are also capable of stopping external bleeding. See **Oak bark**, **Tannic acid jelly**, **Tannic acid**.

Tar A sticky black liquid produced by the destructive dis-tillation of pine wood or coal. Traditionally used mixed with grease as a stopping for hooves and as a dressing for dam-aged feet especially (when mixed with fish oil) for hard and brittle feet. Also, when mixed with cantharides, used for blistering.

Taraxacum officinale see **Dandelion.**

Taxus baccata see **Yew**.

TCM see **Traditional Chinese Medicine.**

Telepathy A method of communication from mind to mind without using known channels of the senses. This form of communication is often used in the diagnosis of physical or mental problems and is gaining in popularity.

Temperature Overall, body temperature is controlled automatically by the brain. However, body heat produced by the muscles increases with exercise and during cold weather, and the body loses heat through evaporation (sweating), via the lungs during increased respiration and through convection conduction, and radiation. Therefore, slight variations in body temperature are normal but, for practical purposes, the usual average temperature of the horse is 100.5 degrees F. (38.0 degrees C.). Temperature-taking is most satisfactorily carried out within the rectum. Unusually high temperatures are associated with the acute stage of disease.

Tendons Fibrous, inelastic pieces of connective tissue, which are attached at one end to the extremities of muscle and at the other to the relevant bone structure. Tendons do not, of themselves, provide the power of contraction, but are simply the means by which the contraction is transferred to the limb. Compare **Ligaments**.

Tenesmus Straining, for example at faeces or urine.

Testicles The male sex organs that produce spermatozoa and androgen. See **Scrotum**.

Tetanus Also known as lockjaw. A specific disease caused by an anaerobic bacterium, *Clostridium tetani*, which is present in most cultivated soils and gains entry to the body through wounds. Deep puncture wounds are more likely to become contaminated than those which are exposed to fresh air. The bacteria produce a powerful toxin, which is absorbed into the general circulatory system, producing stiffness of limbs, etc. However, stiffness of the jaws, which is responsible for the popular name of the disease, is not always seen in the early stages.

Theobromine An alkaline substance found in cocoa. It has a mild diuretic action and also dilates blood vessels. It is a prohibited substance under certain competition rules.

Therapeutic Pertaining to the healing art. See **Medicinal**.

Therapist A person providing therapy. The term, of itself, does not necessarily mean that the person is qualified in any way.

Therapy The treatment of disease. The term is often qualified to limit its range, e.g. physiotherapy, laser therapy, drug therapy, etc.

Thorn apple *(Datura stramonium)* Also known as Jimson weed. An annual plant preferring waste land, tips, etc, introduced to Europe from its native America. Used in medicine as an antispasmodic and in the homoeopathic treatment of convulsions. Thorn apple is listed as a poison — see **Poisonous plants**.

Thoroughpins and windgalls Soft swellings of the joint capsule which appear just above and behind the hock and the fetlock joint respectively. There are several theories as to their exact cause, but they are associated with work in most cases. Apart from being unsightly they are not generally regarded as a problem in themselves. Holistic therapy and nutrition will often help to alleviate them.

Thrush A condition of the foot in which there is inflammation and a foul-smelling discharge. Usually caused by bad management such as dirty stables, bedding etc., and general neglect of the feet.

Ticks Blood-sucking parasitic insects of the order *Acarina*, which live on the skin of horses, most usually appearing between the thighs, under the mane and at the root of the tail.Ticks can be carriers of infectious disease. In common with other parasitic infestations, they are most likely to occur in animals who are neglected. See also **Parasites**.

Timothy *(Phleum pratense)* A species of grass recommended for horse pastures. See **Meadow**.

Tincture A preparation made by steeping plant material in alcohol. The advantages of this method are that the extraction process is very thorough and the end product has a long shelf-life. Materials for popular traditional tinctures included stryax, opium, euphorbium, rhubarb, myrrh, camphor, asafoetida and senna (Daffy's elixir).

Tissue An aggregation of joined cells, specialised to perform a particular function.

Tissue salts Inorganic mineral salts, also known as biochemic tissue salts. Specific imbalances of tissue salts may be associated with particular diseases. Tissue salt therapy, based on a development of homoeopathic principles, makes use of a range of remedies which restore a healthy balance in the body.

Tobacco *(Nicotiana tabacum)* A plant which contains the alkaloid, nicotine. Traditionally used extensively as a diuretic and in the treatment of colic and constipation; also used to dispel worms. Tobacco, which can be very dangerous, was more often used by amateurs than by bona fide farriers or veterinary surgeons.

Tocopherol Vitaimn E – see **Vitamins**.

Tolerance A reduction in the body's response to a substance which normally provokes a reaction. Tolerance to drugs may occur if they are used over a long period.

Tonic A substance which invigorates the body and promotes well-being.

Topical Where a drug or remedy is applied directly to the part being treated.

Tormentil *(Potentilla erecta)* A perennial plant preferring meadows, bogs and heathland, found in Europe, Asia and

North Africa. Traditionally used as an astringent, sometimes mixed with caraway seeds, for the treatment of diarrhoea.

Torpor A state of diminished responsiveness and sluggishness. Symptomatic of certain diseases and some forms of poisoning.

Torsion see **Twisted gut**.

Tourniquet A device, usually made from a cord or tight bandage, which puts pressure on a bleeding artery in order to stem the flow of blood. Because of the risk of damage to the tissues caused by oxygen starvation, tourniquets are no longer recomended as a first aid measure. Direct pressure on the wound is the alternative action.

Tow Fibres of hemp flax or jute, traditionally teased out and used in swabs, etc.

Toxaemia Blood poisoning caused by bacteria which form toxins in a local site of infection. Compare **Septicaemia**.

Toxic Describes an agent which has a potentially lethal effect.

Toxicology The study of poisonous substances and their effects on the body.

Toxin A poisonous substance produced by living organisms, especially bacteria.

Trace elements Substances required by the body in minute amounts. They include arsenic, chromium, cobalt, copper, fluorine, iodine, iron, manganese, molybdenum, nickel, selenium, silicon, tin, vanadium and zinc. They are often seriously depleted from the soil through the use of artificial nitrogenous fertilisers.

Traditional Chinese Medicine For thousands of years,

the most consistently prevalent and popular system of medicine in the world. A medical philosophy based on integrated systems of treatment including holistic therapies such as acupuncture. Some aspects of the modern version are repugnant to people concerned about animal welfare but the overall philosophical, nutritional, herbal and lifestyle aspects are extremely valuable.

Traditional medicine Those forms of medicine practised in communities which are unaffected by modern technology. Plant medicine is by far the most prominent feature. The World Health Organisation is promoting traditional medicine in its programme designed to improve health in the Third World. See **Alternative medicine**, **Complementary medicine**, **Holistic therapy**.

Tragacanth A gum obtained from spiny shrubs of the genus *Astragalus*. Traditionally used for its mucilaginous properties.

Tranquilliser An agent which produces a calming effect. The term usually refers to a drug.

Trauma A wound caused by physical damage, or an event causing a damaging psychological affect which may lead to neurosis.

Trumpeting see **High-blowing**.

Trifolium see **Clover**.

Trigonella foenum-graecum see **Fenugreek**.

Tucked up A term describing the appearance of a horse who has his loins drawn up behind the ribs. It can be a sign of illness, overwork, bad management, etc

Tumour An abnormal swelling in or on the body, which may be either benign or malignant.

Turnip The root of *Brassica rapa*. Traditionally used as an admixture to provide variety to the horse's diet. Turnips must be fed cooked.

Turpentine (oil of) A resinous, oily substance originally obtained from the Terebinth tree (Chian turpentine), but now also from other species. Formerly used as an anthelmintic, which was given after fasting. Also used as a diuretic and to check capilliary bleeding. When mixed with opium, given as a treatment for colic. Turpentine, mixed with mustard or with ammonia and linseed oil, was also administered externally as a counter-irritant.

Tussilago farfara see **Coltsfoot**.

Twisted gut The most dramatic and serious form of colic, in which the intestines become twisted and contorted so as to restrict the blood supply. The horse suffers agony in this condition and emergency surgery is required if he is to survive. See also **Colic**.

I ▶ **Twitch** A device used as a means of restraint, consisting of a short pole with a cord passed through a small hole at one end and then knotted to form a continuous loop. The loop is placed around the upper lip of the horse and tightened by twisting the pole. An alternative method of making a twitch is to pass the cord through a small metal ring which can be held firmly in the hand.

   The calming influence of the twitch is thought to result from its pressure on acupuncture points, which stimulates the release of endorphins into the bloodstream. The same technique is used by hunting pack animals to restrain their prey.

   Properly employed, the twitch is not inhumane, but its use can make some horses head-shy.

Tying- up see **Azoturia**.

Tympany Tight accumulation of gas, for example in the intestines.

Ulcer   An open sore which fails to heal.

Ulmus fulva   see **Slippery elm**.

Ultrasonic therapy   This entails treatment of the body with high-frequency sound pressure waves which are inaudible to the human ear. These are created by subjecting a quartz crystal to an electrical field, which causes it to vibrate and produce the necessary ultrasonic waves. The treatment works by producing vibrations and heat in the tissues, which stimulate healing.

When used as part of a holistic approach to medicine, ultrasound therapy can be very effective, but it is not a system of medicine in its own right. The misapplication of ultrasound equipment can have serious consequences and therefore it should be used only by suitably qualified and experienced practitioners.

Unconsciousness   A condition in which there is no awareness of surroundings, as in sleep. It is deliberately induced by an anaesthetic during surgical operations.

Undershot jaw   A congentital deformity of the jaw, in which the lower incisors overlap the upper ones. The condition is occasionally seen in the horse, in which case the molars have the same abnormality. It is treated by rasping down the crowns of the top incisors from time to time, and keeping the molars level.

Unguent   Ointment.

Urea   The end-product of protein metabolism in the body and a constituent of urine, in which it is excreted.

Urginea maritima   see **Squill**.

Urine   A fluid excreted by the kidneys, containing end-products from the body such as urea and uric acid.

Urtica dioica   see **Nettle**.

Urticaria An allergic reaction in which the skin becomes covered in red, round weals which may vary in size. The skin becomes intensely itchy, and this condition may continue for hours or days. Urticaria is usually caused by sensitivity to certain ingredients in foodstuffs, or by insect stings and bites.

Vaccination A method of producing future protection from a disease by stimulating an antibody response to a particular pathogen. Vaccination against specific diseases is a prerequisite for certain equestrian sports, but it can bring its own problems for sensitive individuals. See **Nosodes**.

Vaccine A preparation of antigenic material that can be used to stimulate an antibody response, thereby producing a measure of protection against specific diseases. Some sensitive animals can react badly to vaccines. See **Nosodes**.

Vaccinosis Disease resulting from vaccination.

Valerian *(Valeriana officinalis)* A perennial plant, found throughout most of Europe, preferring open woodland, wet meadows, ditches and riverbanks. Valerian is a potent sedative and is used regularly in poly-herbal mixtures sold for calming horses down. It can also be used medically, together with other herbs, for calming digestive upsets caused by nervous tension. Valerian should not be used on a regular basis without veterinary advice.

Vaseline The trade name of an ointment consisting mainly of petroleum jelly. Vaseline replaced animal fats as the basis of many remedies as it did not become rancid. See **Hog's lard**.

Vasodilator A substance that dilates (widens) blood vessels and thus lowers blood pressure.

Vein A blood vessel carrying blood towards the heart. The blood is assisted along its way by one-way valves, which are situated along the walls of the veins. Compare **Artery**.

Ventilation Refers to the measures taken to minimise a

build-up of polluted air. Environmental purity and adequate air exchange are inextricably linked; avoiding air pollution is an essential aspect of good management practice in the maintenance of equine health. Good ventilation depends upon a study of air flow and is not necessarily achieved simply by opening a window or door, which can create unhealthy draughts of air.

Verdigris Cupric acetate: the green coating which forms on cupric (copper-based) metals.

Vermifuge A substance that expels worms from the intestine. See also **Anthelmintic**.

Veronica officinalis see **Speedwell**.

Vesicants an old term for an irritant used in blistering — see **Blistering and rowelling**.

Vessel A closed channel or tube conveying body fluid.

Veterinary Medicines Directorate An executive agency of the Ministry of Agriculture Fisheries and Food, responsible for the testing and licensing of veterinary medicines. See **Medicines Acts**.

Veterinary Surgeon A term reserved exclusively for Members or Fellows of the Royal College of Veterinary Surgeons under an Act of Parliament passed in 1844. The purpose of the legislation is to enable those seeking medical assistance for sick animals to distinguish between practitioners trained in veterinary colleges, and the unqualified. Qualified veterinary surgeons may go on to take post-graduate courses in holistic medicine, such as homoeopathy.

There are strict codes of professional conduct which must be observed by veterinary surgeons, and those wishing to employ the services of holistic practitioners should inform the veterinary surgeon attending the case, so that it may be referred. This is normally the best course of action, since the attending practitioner cannot reasonably object to a consultant being called in, who may be nominated by the owner. The other, less desirable, option is to inform the attending veterinary surgeon that his services will no longer be required, before another practitioner is consulted.

Unfortunately, there is a growing number of individuals and companies producing unlicensed and dubious products, who may seek to gain credibility by associating themselves with the veterinary profession. Under the code of conduct laid down by the Royal College, veterinary surgeons are not allowed to endorse or associate themselves with any commercial product. Those who do so are liable to disciplinary action, which may lead to withdrawal of the right to practise veterinary medicine.

Veterinary Surgeons Act 1966 This Act makes illegal the diagnosis and treatment of disease in animals by persons who are not qualified veterinarians.

Viable nutritional profile Describes feedstuffs which meet the holistic nutritional requirements of the species. See **Holistic feeding stuffs and supplements**.

Vice Any form of chronic objectionable behaviour which is acquired by the horse. Vices take many forms including kicking, biting and general viciousness, rearing, bolting, box-walking, crib-biting, wind-sucking, weaving, chewing rugs, dung-eating and bolting food.

Vices may be of physiological origin, for example a horse who rears for no apparent reason may be experiencing pain caused by a badly fitting saddle. Other vices may be fundamentally neurotic. It should be remembered, however, that many horses are kept in circumstances which are largely unnatural, and this predisposes them to both physiological and psychological stresses which can manifest themselves in undesirable behaviour. Generally speaking, the more closely a horse's regime can be tailored to mimic a natural lifestyle, the less likely he is to develop vices. Correct handling, training and feeding also play a part in the prevention of vices.

Vinegar Dilute, impure acetic acid made from wine, beer, etc. Traditionally used as a styptic, and more recently in the treatment of 'bony problems', where it is said to assist in dissolving and dispersing the associated calculus.

Vinegar of cantharides A chemical preparation formerly used externally for the treatment of splints, spavins and chronic sprains.

Virology The study of viruses.

Virulence The capacity of an infectious organism to cause disease.

Virus A minute, disease-producing organism, capable of replication only within living cells. All viruses are smaller than the smallest bacterium — compare **Bacteria**.

Viscera The organs within the body, especially those of digestion.

Vitamins Fragile, yet potent, chemical compounds required by the body for normal functioning. The term vitamin was first used by a Polish chemist, Casimir Funk in 1911, being derived from 'vita' (life), and 'amine' (substance, incorrectly assigned to all vitamins). Vitamins are, in fact, so different from one another that a providing a meaningful common discription is difficult. They can, however, be conveniently separated into two groups; water-soluble and fat-soluble.

Apart from the vitamins of which we know most, such as A, the B Complex, C, D, E and K, there is a host of others about which we know little, and there are probably many more to be identified. Vitamins are known to be important to the sophisticated chemical processes associated with many complex bodily functions, such as sexual development and reproduction.

Although the existence of vitamins was known before Funk's work, their importance was emphasised by the rise of the modern food industry. As science progressed, it became possible to manufacture vitamins and other micronutrients, which could be used to fortify denatured raw materials.

Vitamins should, however, be provided as an integral part of the horse's diet, and not added as manufactured products, as they are in the majority of compound horse feeds. This is because artificial vitamins are not absorbed by the body either so well, or in the same way as, integral vitamins. Also, their use probably upsets the overall nutrient balance. See also **Additives**, **Holistic feeding stuffs and supplements, Inverted nutrition**, **Non-constituent ingredients**, **Nutrititional supplements**.

Volatile   Describes a liquid which evaporates at room temperature.

Volatile oils see **Aromatherapy**.

Vomit   To eject matter from the stomach, via the mouth. Horses does not normally vomit, in the generally accepted meaning of the word, for anatomical reasons. If a horse appears to vomit this indicates that a serious internal problem has developed and veterinary assistance must be obtained without delay.

Voluntary muscles   Muscles which are under voluntary control, for example those concerned with the movement of the limbs — compare **Involuntary muscles**.
Vulnerary   The name given to substance (particularly in herbal medicine) that promotes wound healing.

Wall-eye   Describes an eye which has lack of pigment in the iris, giving it pinkish-white or blueish-white appearance. The condition is not indicative of blindness.

Warts   Usually small, harmless growths which occur on the surface of the skin. Warts are caused by a virus and often disappear of their own accord. On some parts of the body, such as the penis or lips, they may be troublesome and require veterinary attention.

Water   Absorbed into the body from food as well as being drunk, water accounts for a very large proportion of the horse's bodyweight. It is vital to life, permeating all the tissues of the body, and the importance of its quality is often overlooked.

In addition to being either 'hard' or 'soft', natural water supplies are also open to contamination from many sources, such as farm chemicals, sewage, industial waste, or seepage from land-fill sites. Even minor levels of contamination may have a significant effect on the horse's health: the BAHNM can arrange for water testing to be carried out. Tap water is a different matter, but it will still vary in chemical make-up at different times of the year and according to the area from which it comes.

A constant supply of clean, fresh water must always be available for the horse. Automatic drinkers are very useful and save a lot of time but, as with buckets, they must be kept clean, and their correct functioning must be checked periodically. Plastic containers may not suit all horses.

Wax White and yellow wax was traditionally used to thicken ointments and stiffen plasters without making them brittle. See **Plasters (medicinal)**.

Weal A reddened or pale raised area of the skin of temporary nature, which may be itchy. Weals may be a sign of local or general allergy. See **Urticaria**.

Weaning The time during which a foal ceases to be totally dependent on the mother's milk. Weaning usually takes place between the fourth and sixth week of the foal's life, but this can vary according to circumstances.

Wheat Any cereal grass of the genus *Triticum*. Sometimes used as part of compound rations, together with other high-energy ingredients.

Whisky A grain spirit traditionally used in the treatment of shock and as a stimulant; also for colic and in the treatment of pneumonia.

White Bryony see **Bryony, white**.

White line On the ground surface of the sole of the foot, the union between the sole and the wall is marked by a narrow band of slightly pliable, waxy horn known as the white line. This serves as a guide for the farrier; nails should not be driven inside the line, since this area of the foot is sensitive.

I ▶ **Willow** *(Salix alba)* A deciduous tree, preferring damp locations, found throughout Britain and in central and southern Europe.Willow bark is a source of salicin (also contained in the flower buds of the meadowsweet). It is used in medicine as an anti-inflammatory and analgesic.

Windgalls see **Thoroughpins and windgalls**.

Wintergreen oil An aromatic stimulating oil made from a plant of the genus *Gaultheria* and also from a species of birch. Traditionally used as a linament in the treatment of stiffness and sprains, particularly of the limbs. A synthesised version (methyl salicylate) is sold as 'oil of wintergreen'.

Winter's bark The bark of a South American tree *(Drimys winteri)*, formerly used as a stimulant aromatic tonic. Named after a Captain Winter, who introduced it to England in 1579.

Witch hazel *(Hamamelis virginiana)* A small deciduous tree, preferring damp woodland, found throughout eastern and central North America. Used medicinally in the treatment of bruises and various forms of bleeding: traditionally used to arrest bleeding from wounds, and given internally for haemorrhage from the lungs and abdominal organs.

Woody nightshade see **Bittersweet**.

Worms Intestinal parasites of various types which depend upon the horse as a host for part of their life-cycle. There are many different types of worm including redworms, lungworms, pinworms, hairworms, tapeworms, threadworms and bots. Their presence and activities can make a horse lose general condition, and they are associated with diarrhoea, loss of appetite and colic. Severe infestations can be very serious; severe damage to the horse's internal organs or blood vessels may be irreparable.

There are pharmaceutical wormers available to kill the parasites, but these can bring problems for sensitive animals. It is advisable to test dung samples for evidence of worms before resorting to chemical treatments. Holistic nutrition and good horse and pasture management can prove very effective in reducing the overall worm burden in an equestrian establishment. See **Anthelmintic**.

Wormwood *(Artemisia absinthium)* A perennial plant, preferring a maritime environment, found in Britain, mainland Europe and throughout many other parts of the world. Traditionally used in the treatment of digestive problems and also as an anthelmintic. Once used in the drink, absinthe, but banned because of its toxic effect.

Wort A nutritious liquid made from hops and sometimes malt liquor; a traditional drink for convalescent horses. See also **Malt liquor**.

Wound A break in the surface of the skin, or damage to the structure of an organ. Wounds can be classified into four types:
1) Incised wounds, which are usually inflicted with a sharp instrument such as a knife.
2) Punctured wounds, which are usually inflicted by a sharp-pointed instrument such as a stick or metal spike. Nails from a cast shoe can also inflict such wounds in the sole of the foot.
3) Lacerated wounds; in which there is a high degree of tearing of the flesh; such as may be caused to the legs when a horse falls on a hard surface.
4) Contused wounds, in which there is a high degree of bruising to the surrounding tissue, such as may be caused by a blow from a blunt instrument or by kicks from other horses.

The response of wounds to homoeopathic or herbal medicines without antibiotics is usually very satisfactory.

X-Rays Electromagnetic radiation of extremely short wavelength. X-radiation penetrates matter and acts on photographic film to produce 'x-rays', which have many uses in diagnostic medicine. X-rays are damaging to tissue, and can be used therapeutically to treat certain cancers.

Yarrow *(Achillea millefolium)* A perennial plant reaching about 60cm in height, preferring grassy places, meadows, roadsides and gardens. Found in most parts of Europe, yarrow is used medicinally for digestive problems, and also for the homoeopathic treatment of internal bleeding. Recommended for horse pastures — see **Meadow**.

Yew *(Taxus baccata)* An evergreen tree, native to Britain, growing to 20m in height and preferring chalky soil. It has, for centuries, been cultivated in gardens throughout Britain as an ornamental and hedge plant. Yew contains toxins which are rapidly absorbed from the digestive tract and interfere with the action of the heart. Apart from the potential danger of eating the growing plant, garden refuse containing yew should be avoided, as the toxicity of the plant is not reduced by wilting or drying. Yew is one of the most common causes of serious or fatal poisoning in horses.

Yin—Yang The vital balancing principles of Chinese philosophy and medicine. In times of good health the body's energy, or Qi (pronounced 'chee'), is considered to be in balance in terms of Yin and Yang, which are polar opposites. Disease is seen to be a manifestation of an imbalance of Qi. See **Acupunture, Qi**.

Zedoary An aromatic bitter, obtained from the root of a species of the ginger family which is native to China and India. Traditionally used for the treatment of digestive problems.

Zinc A trace element available in the horse's natural diet, quantities varying amongst individual foods. Associated with cell metabolism.

Zingibar officinale see **Ginger**.

Acorns

Acupuncture Needle

Alder Buckthorn

Arnica

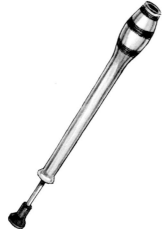

Balling Gun

*Belladonna
(Deadly Nightshade)*

*Bittersweet
(Woody Nightshade)*

Bladderwrack

Broom

Bryony (Black)

Bryony (White)

Burdock (Greater)

Calabar Bean

Chamomile

Comfrey

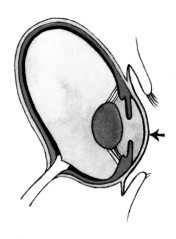

Cornea

Dandelion

Devil's Claw

Elder

Eohippus

Ergot

Ergot

Fenugreek

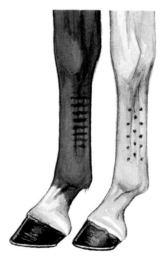

Line and pin firing

Foxglove

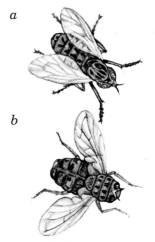

(a) *Gadfly*
(b) *Bot fly*

Hawthorn

Hemlock

Hops

Indian Hemp

Iris (Foetida)

Juniper

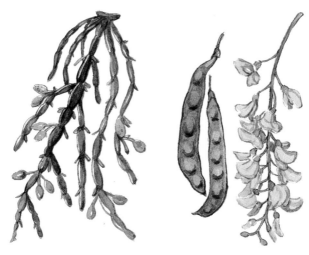

Kelp

Laburnum

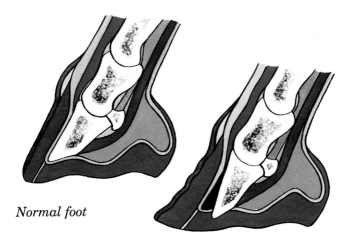

Normal foot

Laminitic foot

209

Licorice

Male Fern

Marigold

Mint

Monk's hood

Nettles

Nux Vomica

Over-reach

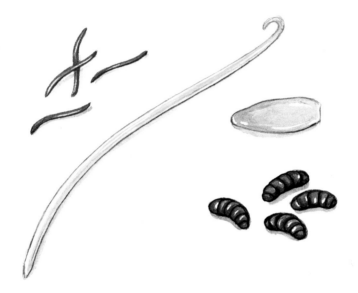

Parasites

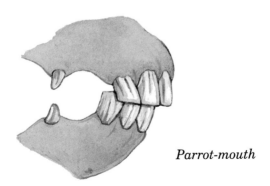

Parrot-mouth

Photosensitivity

Poppies

Rhododendron

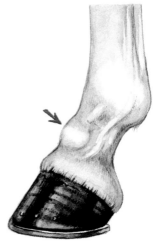

Ringbone

213

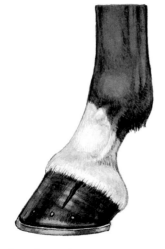

Sand crack

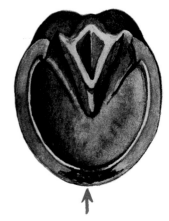

Seedy toe

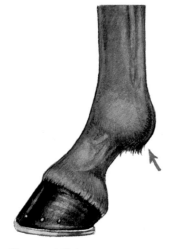

Sesamoiditis

Spavin

St John's Wort

Stringhalt

Twitch

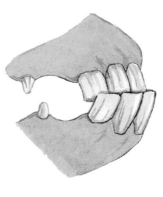

Undershot Jaw

Valerian

Wall-eye

Willow

Yew